*Dr. Millicent Hunter*

## 40-Day Journal

# Don't Die in the Winter…

### *Your Season Is Coming*

## DR. MILLICENT HUNTER

D0815892

Text compiled by Jan Sherman.

## Destiny Image₍®₎ Publishers, Inc.
P.O. Box 310
Shippensburg, PA 17257-0310

*"Speaking to the Purposes of God for This Generation
and for the Generations to Come"*

ISBN 0-7684-2314-7

For Worldwide Distribution
Printed in the U.S.A.

This book and all other Destiny Image, Revival Press, MercyPlace,
Fresh Bread, Destiny Image Fiction, and Treasure House books are available
at Christian bookstores and distributors worldwide.

1 2 3 4 5 6 7 8 9 10 /11 10 09 08 07 06 05

For a U.S. bookstore nearest you,  call
**1-800-722-6774.**

For more information on foreign distributors, call
**717-532-3040.**

Or reach us on the Internet:
**www.destinyimage.com**

# Table of Contents

# Our God Is a Seasonal God

T O EVERY THING THERE IS A SEASON, AND A TIME TO EVERY PURPOSE UNDER THE HEAVEN (ECCLESIASTES 3:1).

*I* had a vision and a directive from God for this new ministry. Instead of the fruitful blessings I expected, however, the Spirit of God led me into the wilderness, into a spiritual season, where I met my enemy. I learned to survive the cold, the depth, the dry places, and the hopelessness of winter.

In spite of the harsh winter winds, I knew that my "season of fruitfulness" was coming. I could not afford to die in the winter and miss God. I had to learn how to protect myself against the deadly elements that attacked my ministry, my home, my family, and my physical body.

I could still hear the Holy Spirit speaking, *"Don't die in the winter; don't give up; spring is coming...."*

All through the Body of Christ, Christians are learning to understand, prepare for, and endure their spiritual winters. Our lives are in a process of continual change. Although God is the same yesterday, today, and forever, He is continually transforming us. Paul tells us that "we...are changed into the same image from glory to glory, even as by the Spirit of the Lord" (2 Cor. 3:18).

There is a right time for everything, and everything has its season. The secret to peace in God is to discover, expect, and appreciate God's perfect timing in your life.

(Quote from *Don't Die in the Winter*, Pages 18-19)

# QUESTIONS

1. Did God ever ask you to do something and when you obeyed by faith, you found yourself in a spiritual wilderness instead of a fruitful time of blessing? What does God teach us during wilderness times?

2. What types of harsh winds have you experienced in a season of winter in your life? What kinds of things protect us from these spiritual winters?

3. Have you experienced a spiritual winter but knew that a new season of spring was coming? How can we see beyond our dire circumstances so that we can find hope of fruitfulness in the season ahead?

4. At this point in your life, what do you know to do to understand, prepare for, and endure spiritual winters? How easy has it been to accept the changes winters bring to you?

5. How does discovering, expecting, and appreciating God's perfect timing bring peace to your life? How satisfied are you with God's sovereignty in terms of how He brings seasons of winter and spring to you?

# MEDITATION

*"Every living thing passes through seasons of change.*
*Some seasons are easy, even pleasant, to pass through.*
*Others are very difficult. Our God is a seasonal God"*

(*Don't Die in the Winter,* Page 19).


*Think about a season of time that was*
*very pleasant or easy for you to go through.*
*Then remember one that was more difficult.*
*How have these seasons affected your outlook on life?*

# Life Changes Teach Us

THOU HAST COVERED ME IN MY MOTHER'S WOMB. I WILL PRAISE THEE; FOR I AM FEARFULLY AND WONDERFULLY MADE... (PSALM 139:13B-14).

## ☙ Today's Devotion ❧

ot only are there seasons in the natural realm, but we have seasons in our physical lives as well. From the moment we are conceived in our mother's womb, a human growth cycle is set in motion, one that brings about certain biological changes. This growth cycle is separated into specific divisions much like seasons.

This cycle is governed and characterized by the development and the maturity of the various body systems. The cells multiply and they become a zygote. This completes a season. The zygote then becomes an embryo and that is a season.

Our growth cycle does not stop with the initial stages of fetal development, however. Every millisecond of our existence, from birth to childhood, adulthood to death, we are constantly changing.

We are different in some way today from what we were yesterday. There will be something different about each individual tomorrow that is not evident today. Some of these changes are so very subtle that they go completely unnoticed and undetected, but they are there.

One hundred hairs fell out of our head yesterday. One thousand skin cells fell off of our upper epidermal layer this morning…. Every moment of our lives we are changing.

(Quote from *Don't Die in the Winter,* Pages 20-21)

# QUESTIONS

1. How do seasons of change in our physical bodies affect us emotionally? How do they affect us spiritually?

2. Just as the physical body's cycles include development and maturity, how do you think spiritual cycles include development and maturity?

3. Do you like change? Why or why not? What conditions make change easy for you to accept? What makes them more difficult?

4. Because we are constantly changing physically, how do those physical changes contribute to how we act or react to situations or people?

5. Science proves that some of our physical changes are so subtle they go undetected. Do some emotional changes follow suit? What about spiritual changes?

## MEDITATION

*"Sometimes change is upsetting and disquieting because it disturbs the boundaries of our comfort zone. In our comfort zone we know what is coming next. There is no need to be on guard or to watch our backs. We just 'go with the flow.' Life is comfortable"*

(*Don't Die in the Winter*, Page 21).

*What is your comfort zone? Describe its boundaries in terms of physical, emotional, and spiritual elements. What boundaries are easy to change and which are more difficult?*

# Passing Through Spiritual Seasons

REMEMBER YE NOT THE FORMER THINGS, NEITHER CONSIDER THE THINGS OF OLD. BEHOLD, I WILL DO A NEW THING; NOW IT SHALL SPRING FORTH; SHALL YE NOT KNOW IT? I WILL EVEN MAKE A WAY IN THE WILDERNESS, AND RIVERS IN THE DESERT (ISAIAH 43:18-19).

Those of us who are spiritually sensitive are keenly aware of a tremendous moving and shaking taking place in the Body of Christ. A great deal of the status quo is changing. Traditions and customs are changing. Old habits, practices, rules, and regulations are coming under close scrutiny, and change is evident....

God prepares His people to do battle with the enemy. This preparation molds us, makes us, designs us, and shapes us. In the process we are pruned, tested, and tried in order to conform to the image of His Son....

Many Christians are going through situations that are very difficult to understand. But just as there are seasons and specific times of growth and development in the human body, so there are seasons, or specific times of growth and development, in our spiritual lives....

Most of us want to believe that if the Holy Spirit is leading us, He will always lead us beside still waters. But, just like Jesus, sometimes the Holy Spirit leads us into dry and desolate places where there is no rest, relief, or comfort. It is a spiritual season that we must pass through, just as Jesus did.

(Quote from *Don't Die in the Winter,* Pages 22-23)

# QUESTIONS

1. Have you noticed a tremendous moving and shaking taking place in the Body of Christ? What kinds of things have you seen?

2. How does the moving and shaking in the Body prepare God's people to do battle? Why do we need to conform to His image in order to face the enemy?

3. Are you or is someone you know going through a situation that is difficult to understand? What makes it difficult? How are these difficult times part of our growth and development?

4. If the Holy Spirit is our Teacher, why doesn't He always lead us beside still waters? When would the Holy Spirit lead us to such a restful place?

5. Why does the Holy Spirit lead us to desolate places? What did Jesus learn in the wilderness? Are these lessons we must learn as well?

## ⮜ MEDITATION ⮞

*"We experience the full depth of all four seasons
in our spiritual growth. So if we are to mature in the
things of God, we need to adapt to seasonal changes"*

(Don't Die in the Winter, Page 22).


*What does this mean? What is necessary in
our lives to be in the "ready position" to adapt?*

# Why Are Spiritual Winters Necessary?

Though now for a season, if need be, ye are in heaviness through manifold temptations (1 Peter 1:6).

*W*inter does not stay all year long. Spring is just around the corner. We have got to learn how to hang in there because it is only for a season. You must understand that trials will come your way.

We must learn how to adapt to seasonal changes. We have to prepare for and protect ourselves from spiritual winters just as we do from the dangers of natural winters. The perils and pitfalls of seasonal changes must be resisted.

The devil knows us and he knows all about us. He knows whether or not we have established a pattern of resistance. Just as a weak body catches a cold easily, we can catch all kinds of illnesses that are spiritually-oriented when our spiritual resistance is low.

Some of us are overtaken by every little thing in our life and we are susceptible to everything that the enemy does. Some of us have been suffering through some difficult things in our lives for a very long time—in fact, it has been so long that we think suffering is a way of life.... But God says, *"I gave unto you power and it's up to you to tell the devil 'I take authority over you' when you want him to leave you alone."*

The battleground, you see, is in your mind.

(Quote from *Don't Die in the Winter,* Pages 30-31)

# QUESTIONS

1. When you are waiting for a Spring to come, how do you "hang in there"? What are some promises in the Word that help keep you looking forward?

2. Does knowing the fact that trials will come your way help you keep from being taken by surprise when difficulties occur? How can you protect and prepare yourself for spiritual winters?

3. What are some spiritually-oriented diseases? Are there specific spiritual diseases that seem to come your way more often than others? What lowers your spiritual resistance?

4. Which best describes you—overtaken by every little thing and susceptible to everything the enemy does, or suffering through difficult things for a very long time? Why do you think you are weak in the way you have chosen to describe yourself? How can you resist this?

5. How does power and authority dispel long-term suffering? Why is the battleground in our minds?

# MEDITATION

*"If we tell Jesus, 'Nobody knows the trouble I've seen,'*
*Jesus says, 'I do; I've been there.' " Do you ever get*
*the woe-is-me blues? Do you ever ask God, "Why me?"*

(*Don't Die in the Winter,* Page 26).

*Why is this the wrong question to ask?*

# Spring Will Come

FOR THOUGH WE WALK IN THE FLESH, WE DO NOT WAR AFTER THE FLESH: (FOR THE WEAPONS OF OUR WARFARE ARE NOT CARNAL, BUT MIGHTY THROUGH GOD TO THE PULLING DOWN OF STRONG HOLDS.) (2 CORINTHIANS 10:3-4).

*A*fter you have come through great turmoil and great suffering, you will see a ray of sunshine and begin to feel the refreshing power of God....

God is watching you. He is waiting to see what you are going to do. God has to know that He can trust you. Some of you are losing your conviction and compromising your faith. You are sitting down, giving up, and dying in the winter.

God chooses our time of blessing. He knows just when to bless us, where to bless us, and how to bless us. Perhaps you have been praying about something for days, weeks, months, or years, but God has not brought it to pass yet. You feel like you are in the valley of the shadow of death; you feel as if you are having a wilderness experience....

The Spirit of God has *led* you to a time of testing and trials so when He does bless you and bring you forth, you will be anointed with all power and authority on earth. *"Don't die in the winter!"*

The Spirit of the Lord is saying, *"Get up, square your shoulders, clear your head, and praise Me! Walk like you have the victory because your season of blessing is coming."*

(Quote from *Don't Die in the Winter,* Pages 31, 33-34)

# QUESTIONS

1. How do you establish a pattern of resistance to the devil? Rate yourself on how well you do the following:

   - Put on the full armor of God (see Eph. 6:13-17).

   - Protect yourself with the Word of God (see Eph. 6:17b; 2 Tim. 3:16-17; Heb. 4:12).

   - Prepare yourself with prayer (see Eph. 6:18; Phil. 4:6).

   - Learn how to praise Him at all times (see Phil. 4:4; Eph. 5:19-20).

   - Submit yourself to God, resist satan, and he will run from you (see Jas. 4:7).

2. Have you ever come through a trial and felt the refreshing power of God? What made the change for you?

3. Why does God watch and wait to see what we will do during our difficult experiences? Why is trust such an important element in times of testing?

4. Have you ever lost your conviction and felt like giving up? What wore you down to this point? What does God offer us so that we are able to get up and trust Him again?

5. How does praising God before our blessing arrives demonstrate our trust in God? How do you walk in victory before you experience the victory?

## ☙ MEDITATION ☚

*"I refuse to die because I know that the blessing is coming.
I have seen the seasonal cycle take place in my own life
and ministry. I know that springtime always follows winter"*

(*Don't Die in the Winter*, Page 33).

*The author is firm with this resolve. How firm are
you to say the same about your life? What makes
the difference to be able to speak so confidently?*

# The Four Seasons in Your Life

FOR THE INVISIBLE THINGS OF HIM FROM THE CREATION OF THE WORLD ARE CLEARLY SEEN, BEING UNDERSTOOD BY THE THINGS THAT ARE MADE, EVEN HIS ETERNAL POWER AND GODHEAD... (ROMANS 1:20).

## ☙ TODAY'S DEVOTION ☙

Something...usually happens during the first springtime of our spiritual lives. When we plant a seed prayer, and it is watered and cultivated—it ultimately develops into our life focus for God, or our "calling." We might begin to ask the Lord to "use us for His glory," or to "give us a burden for souls."...These prayers are seeds that need to mature with the passing seasons of our lives....

The light and warmth of the summer sun helps the seedling to continue to grow to a sapling. Summers are filled with activity. People feel very much alive.... I have had these times in my life; just me and Jesus, Jesus and me. I had no bills, no problems, and no major decisions to make....

Pruning takes place in the fall. Orchard growers prune or cut back the branches to remove the superfluous branches. This improves the shape of the tree, encourages growth, increases fruitfulness, and makes the fruit easier to reach. Each season of pruning produces growth.

The maturity of a tree can be determined by counting the rings in the trunk. These rings are markings that say, "This tree went through a period of successful growth. It endured the adversity of winter weather and environmental conditions and survived."

(Quote from *Don't Die in the Winter*, Pages 38-41)

## QUESTIONS

1. Do you remember the first springtime of your spiritual life? What seed prayers did you plant? Did you discover your "calling" at this time?

2. What seeds did you plant early in your walk with Christ that have matured with the passing seasons of your life? Which have grown into fruitful trees?

3. Reflect on a summer in your spiritual life. What activities made it alive for you? What was your relationship with Jesus like?

4. Describe a season of autumn in your spiritual life. What did God prune in order to increase your growth?

5. If your spiritual life could be examined like the cross section of a tree trunk, how many rings would be found? How would each ring reflect the four seasons of your spiritual life?

## MEDITATION

*"God has always used the pictures of nature to tell us about Himself, His character, and even ourselves. Creation itself reveals what God is like. All we have to do is to look very closely at the things He has put in front of us"*

(*Don't Die in the Winter*, Page 37).

*If you were to describe what God is like using one object of nature, what would you choose? What would your description include that would help reveal who He is to a nonbeliever?*

# Jesus Is the Vine

I AM THE TRUE VINE, AND MY FATHER IS THE HUSBANDMAN. EVERY BRANCH IN ME THAT BEARETH NOT FRUIT HE TAKETH AWAY: AND EVERY BRANCH THAT BEARETH FRUIT, HE PURGETH IT, THAT IT MAY BRING FORTH MORE FRUIT (JOHN 15:1-2).

# ❧ TODAY'S DEVOTION ❧

*T*he branches all claim to be followers of Christ. However, the fruitful branches are true believers who, by their living union with Christ, produce much fruit. But the unproductive branches...will be separated from the Vine....They will be cut off and cast aside.

When a vine bears "much fruit," God is glorified because He has sent the sunshine and rain to make the crop grow. He has constantly nurtured the tiny plant and prepared it to blossom. When the fruit harvest comes, the Lord of the harvest is glorified....

During the pruning process a tree often bleeds sap. The caretaker binds up the open branches so the tree will remain strong. The sap itself solidifies and acts like a bandage over the open cut....

In the Christian life, branches can be characteristic of our spiritual development in specific areas. One branch represents our love for others. One is forgiveness, one is mercy, and another is generosity. Each one of these branches must be pruned by God. Just as a caretaker prunes a tree, God allows us to be cut by circumstances in particular areas of our life. This is necessary for greater growth in those areas and, thereby, for greater potential for ministry.

(Quote from *Don't Die in the Winter,* Pages 42-43)

# QUESTIONS

1. How easy is it for you to distinguish between fruitful branches and unproductive branches? Why is it so imperative that branches produce fruit?

2. What fruit are you currently producing? Are you producing "much fruit" or merely a scattering of fruit? Where have you blossomed the most in your fruitfulness?

3. Where have you had the greatest harvest? How was the Lord glorified in what you produced?

4. Think back to a time of pruning in your life. Did you seem to "bleed" when cut? How did God, the Vinedresser, care for you so that you would remain strong?

5. Name some of the spiritual branches under development within you. What is their current condition? Which branches are being cut by circumstances you are facing today? What promise do you have before you that gives you hope during this pruning process?

## MEDITATION

*"Jesus tells us that He is the Vine and the Father is the Vinegrower who cares for the branches to make them fruitful"*

(*Don't Die in the Winter*, Page 42).

*How well connected are you to the Vine? What are some specific ways the Vinegrower has cared for you?*

# *Winter*

THE LORD GOD IS MY STRENGTH, AND HE WILL MAKE MY FEET LIKE HINDS' FEET, AND HE WILL MAKE ME TO WALK UPON MINE HIGH PLACES... (HABAKKUK 3:19).

*T*he scheme of creation prepares the tree by dropping its leaves and pulling all of its life resources deep into the branches, trunk, and roots. Winter is not a time of growth for the tree; it is a time of endurance and testing. If the roots have sunk deeply enough, if its overall health is good, and if the young tree is given adequate protection by the farmer, it will survive the chilly winds of winter and the cold blanket of snow.

It began to snow in my life. The weather turned cold, the sky gray, and the outlook bleak....I told God, "Lord, I want hinds' feet on high places! I want more of You!"...

The Lord showed me that there are many who desire to walk forward in Christ, but there are few who are willing to climb as well. Climbing requires effort. You have to hoist yourself up and exert energy in order to climb....

In the natural, even though everything appears to be cold and dead, if you dig down through the snow and the dirt deep enough, you will find life. The insects, moles, and squirrels are still there. The plants are dormant, but they are alive and they will bloom again in the spring.

(Quote from *Don't Die in the Winter*, Pages 46, 49)

## QUESTIONS

1. If God has prepared seasons of spiritual winters for us, why do most Christians dislike them? Is it hard for you to eagerly embrace this season? Why or why not?

2. How well rooted are you to endure your next winter? Is your overall spiritual health good enough to weather its bleak conditions? Has the Farmer given you adequate protection to survive?

3. High places are usually treacherous, cold, and windy. Why do hinds choose mountains for their habitat? What do they need to survive? What do you need?

4. Mountains are also places where the view is spectacular but you must climb to get there. What does spiritual climbing involve? Are you strong enough for your next climb?

5. Digging through the snow of circumstances in your life takes a tool. What is it? When you have the faith to dig, what might you find while waiting for spring to come?

## ≈ MEDITATION ≈

*"Winter is inevitable in the life of every believer, and the first bitter experience is often the most difficult one to pass through"*

(Don't Die in the Winter, Page 46).

*Do you remember your first (or an early) spiritual winter? What were the elements that made it difficult to pass through? What did you learn on the other side?*

# God Is Not Surprised

MY BRETHREN, COUNT IT ALL JOY WHEN YE FALL INTO DIVERS TEMP-TATIONS; KNOWING THIS, THAT THE TRYING OF YOUR FAITH WORKETH PATIENCE. BUT LET PATIENCE HAVE HER PERFECT WORK, THAT YE MAY BE PERFECT AND ENTIRE, WANT-ING NOTHING (JAMES 1:2-4).

*G*od...is not "caught off guard" by anything that happens in your life. God thinks about you 24 hours a day....

It is mind-boggling to me to know that, right now, this moment, God is thinking about me. When I am asleep, He is thinking about me. He is thinking about you too. Even though we must take responsibility for our own choices in life, it is a comfort to know that God can take even our bad choices and cause them to work for our good....

Many people who live in winter climates actually enjoy the season because they learn to protect themselves from its negative effects. They ski, ice skate, and sled down snowy slopes....The cold frigid air actually *invites* vacationers. They are *prepared* for winter.

We too must be spiritually prepared to protect ourselves from the negative effects of a harsh winter. Our preparations do not stop the season from coming, but they do protect us from devastation. We need to be fully clothed in the armor of God (see Eph. 6:10-17) and the garments of salvation and praise (see Is. 61:3,10). If we are properly attired spiritually, then situations and circumstances will not affect us in a negative way.

(Quote from *Don't Die in the Winter,* Pages 51-52)

# QUESTIONS

1. Have you ever felt caught off-guard about circumstances in your life? Did it ever seem that God might be also surprised by your situation? How does this reflect God's sovereignty and His trust-worthiness?

2. Is it overwhelming to consider that God spends 24 hours a day thinking about you? What does this say about your importance to Him? How should this affect you when you feel lonely, afraid, or victimized?

3. How does God make our bad choices work for our good? How can He do this? Does this mean we don't have to worry about our choices? Why or why not?

4. List the hardships of physical winters (cold, snow, etc.) and match them with the benefits of winter (cold = animals hibernate; snow = skiing, etc.). Now do the same exercise for spiritual winters. What benefits mean the most to you?

5. How well are you clothed in the armor of God? Do you utilize the different pieces of armor effectively? How can this prepare you for winter? How does praise bring protection during spiritual winters?

## ☞ | MEDITATION | ☞

*"Whatever it is in your life, you can make it. It is not a surprise to God"*

(*Don't Die in the Winter*, Page 51).

*Think about these statements in terms of your present circumstances. If the author is correct, how will these truths affect your attitudes toward your circumstances?*

# Spiritual Trees Need Living Water

B LESSED IS THE MAN...HIS LEAF ALSO SHALL NOT WITHER; AND WHATSOEVER HE DOETH SHALL PROSPER (PSALM 1:1,3).

## ❧ TODAY'S DEVOTION ❧

One seasonal year passes to the next and each winter promises a new springtime. After our initial springtime in the Lord, we are ready to bloom forth and produce fruit. Each cycle of seasons gives us new strength and Christian maturity.... God is here with us. He is always present, and always preparing us for one more seasonal change so that our roots will dig deeper in Him and we will bear fruit....

As the pastor and shepherd of the people, it is my responsibility to make sure that the river in the midst of the congregation contains pure, unpolluted living water so the spiritual trees can all grow strong, healthy, and vibrant....

...It is as though God has made me a caretaker over this well of Living Water. A good water source is vital to the life and health of everything that is growing.

I must make certain that no one comes along and pollutes this well with anything that is not of God. I must make certain that it is in perfect condition—pure, and untainted for those who are thirsty. God holds me responsible. This is what ministry is all about. We are caretakers of the well of Living Water and God holds us accountable.

(Quote from Don't Die in the Winter, Pages 52-54)

# QUESTIONS

1. If you were to trace your cycles of spiritual seasons, would you see a consistent overall growth in your life? Which areas did you grow more? Which areas need pruning to encourage more growth?

2. Knowing God is always present should help us in each season. In what ways does this fact make a difference in winter? In spring? In summer? In fall?

3. Just as the author saw her responsibility in making sure her congregation drank from Living Water, we should be sure those under our charge do the same. To whom are you responsible for giving Living Water? How can you be sure you are being a good caretaker of this well?

4. How do we prevent pollution from entering our well of Living Water? How do we maintain its purity? What must we do as individuals to maintain perfect conditions for our water source?

5. What does the author mean when she says, "God holds us accountable"? What does this accountability look like? Why is it so important?

# MEDITATION

*"Blessings chase us in our spring season.*
*They hunt us down and pick us out in a crowd.*
*During our spiritual springtime, our cup overflows with*
*joy until we are laughing and crying at the same time"*

(*Don't Die in the Winter*, Page 54).

*Have you ever felt "chased" by blessings?*
*Reflect on a spring season that was overflowing with*
*joy. What elements created this spiritual springtime?*

# The Season's Best

FOR THE LORD GOD IS A SUN AND SHIELD: THE LORD WILL GIVE GRACE AND GLORY: NO GOOD THING WILL HE WITHHOLD FROM THEM THAT WALK UPRIGHTLY (PSALM 84:11).

*N*atural fruit will not ripen prior to its season. It is not as palatable if it is not given sufficient time to ripen. Restaurant menus have a notation that says, "Certain items can be served only when their fruit is in season." For example, it is not a good thing to order cheesecake with strawberries in the dead of winter. Although strawberries are available in winter, they are not at their peak of perfection. They are not as sweet, as red, as juicy, or as tasty as they are in the height of their season.

When our spiritual fruit comes forth in the right season, everything that we do will prosper. We will prosper because God will open the doors. God will make opportunities that can be made only when His divine hand is in our life. God's methods may change, but His ultimate purpose (that we have an intimate relationship with Him) does not....

Therefore, we must conclude that if God withholds a certain thing that we have been praying for, and He does not bring it forth, then it is no longer working for our good. In other words, there are some blessings that God cannot give us because it is not the right season for that specific blessing.

(Quote from *Don't Die in the Winter*, Pages 58-59)

# QUESTIONS

1. Availability and delectability are dependent upon whether a fruit is in season or not. Have you had fruit in your life that suddenly seemed "out of season" and unavailable for you to use as you had in the past? Have you ever found that what had been fruitful and received well in the Body of Christ became distasteful in another time? Why does this occur? How can we recognize when our fruit is out of season?

2. What are the signs that our fruit is prospering? Reflect on a time when a specific fruit prospered in your life in a way that was miraculous or supernatural.

3. How does producing fruit in season help us reach toward God's ultimate purpose for us? What does intimacy have to do with fruit?

4. Has God ever withheld something from you that you later saw as His wisdom within His timing? How does this apply to fruit that we produce or *try* to produce?

5. What kind of role does God play when we produce fruit? What is our role? How do these roles work together to produce the best fruit in the right season?

*"As human beings, we usually think we need to know what comes next. God does not always make us privy to such information. However, He has promised that if we walk uprightly, He will not withhold any good thing from us"*

(*Don't Die in the Winter*, Page 58).

*Why does God keep some things from us?*
*What does this do for our character?*
*What does it do for our fruit production?*

# The Approach of Seasons

B EHOLD, I WILL DO A NEW THING; NOW IT SHALL SPRING FORTH; SHALL YE NOT KNOW IT? (ISAIAH 43:19A)

## TODAY'S DEVOTION

*G*od has also promised us that we will be able to recognize the approach of seasons and know when new things are about to spring forth....

There are three ways that we can recognize the approach of our blessed season.

1. God plants us in a stable and secure place.

2. Our inner clock is set for a divine appointment.

3. The enemy comes in like a flood.

Even if you do not know what the future holds, you know that God has promised you certain things in His Word. So if you hold on to His promises, then God can develop the character in you that is necessary to thrive in the ministry that He calls you to.

Your heart should be thumping in your chest...knowing that God will soon bring about a great harvest in your life.

...Sometimes the devil actually recognizes the approach of our season before we do. This is why it is so important for us to understand the seasonal nature of God....

We cannot pray away God's seasons. The Lord has a purpose in appointing only certain seasons for fruitfulness.

Natural plants are not fruitful all the time. The evergreen tree seems to be in its fullest bloom all the time, but actually, it is the healthiest in the wintertime.

(Quote from *Don't Die in the Winter*, Pages 59, 61)

# QUESTIONS

1. Has God ever planted you in a stable and secure place to usher in a season of blessing? How did it make you feel? What happened spiritually?

2. Have you ever felt that God was setting your inner clock for a divine appointment? Have circumstances ever come quickly to show you His hand was setting you up for increased blessing? What effect did this have on you spiritually?

3. Have you had a time that the enemy came in like a flood and you knew God was preparing you for something great? Did you have the faith to see beyond your challenges? How did this affect you spiritually?

4. How do you hold on to the promises of God? How does God develop your character to thrive in the ministry He has called you to? Do you anticipate the season of blessing with emotion?

5. Preparation for a time of fruitfulness and blessing is necessary. Why? Just as we see God's hand in our lives in seasons of fall and winter, why do we need to see God's hand in spring and summer?

# MEDITATION

*"God is preparing us to be a blessing to Him and to others. God knows that the real challenge is to produce quality and not quantity. As we recognize the approach of our season, we should celebrate what God is about to do in our life"*

(*Don't Die in the Winter*, Page 60).

*Are you actively exercising this principle in your life? How do you celebrate what God is about to do?*

# Blessings Will Come

H AVING DONE ALL, TO STAND (EPHESIANS 6:13B).

*G*od...will open doors for you. He will not only open doors, but God will cut doors out of brick walls and enable you to go through situations that, in the natural, would be impossible for you to handle. But God will bless you and cause all things to work in obedience *when it is time for Him to activate certain blessings in your life.*

There is what I call a "best time." When we look at flowers, fruits, and vegetables in the natural, there is always a "best time" for each thing growing in nature. Today, though, we are at such a level in our technological growth that we can produce any kind of flower, fruit, or vegetable 12 months out of a year by using certain kinds of lamps, artificial lighting, and the hothouse environment....

There is something about a tomato that ripens in the beautiful bright sunshine of a July summer that cannot be duplicated in a hothouse situation. Although that hothouse tomato is a good tomato and can be used effectively for certain purposes, it has not been allowed to ripen to its best time. Any other time is "a time," but it is not the "best time."

(Quote from *Don't Die in the Winter,* Pages 63-64)

# QUESTIONS

1. Has God ever opened doors for you that could not have been opened any other way? When He did this, were there specific lessons He wanted you to learn?

2. Has God ever enabled you to have the strength to go through situations that would have been impossible for you to handle in the natural? When He provides this kind of strength, what does He teach us?

3. Why is obedience such a major factor in order for God to activate certain blessings in your life? Is it your obedience alone or are others part of His obedience factor?

4. What is a "best time" in the spiritual sense? Have you seen God produce "best times" in your life? What were their purposes?

5. How can we gain patience to "ripen" our fruit in the proper timing of God? What other fruit of the Spirit can help us produce the best fruit at the right time?

## MEDITATION

*"We must grow consistently, and we must
grow at a rate that God has set. Therefore,
God specifically designs and allows things
to occur in our lives so the maximum
amount of spiritual growth will take place
before He activates His blessings and our call"*

(Don't Die in the Winter, Page 64).

*Think of God as your personal trainer.
How does His maximum-effectiveness
program prepare you for fruitfulness?*

# A Season of Pain for a Season of Gain

BLESSED IS THE MAN WHOSE STRENGTH IS IN THEE; IN WHOSE HEART ARE THE WAYS OF THEM. WHO PASSING THROUGH THE VALLEY OF BACA MAKE IT A WELL; THE RAIN ALSO FILLETH THE POOLS (PSALM 84:5-6).

*W*e sing a song in Baptist congregations with a chorus section, "No cross, no crown." The world often says, "No pain, no gain."

A season of pain is necessary because it produces patience and longsuffering, gives us a heart of compassion, deepens our awareness of who God is in our life, and gives us hope. It changes our focus, not so much to particular circumstances and situations, but teaches us and trains us to keep our focus on God and His power in our life.

Unfortunately, so many of these wonderful attributes can be acquired only through painful and difficult situations in our life. That, however, is just the way that God designed it.

When I encounter a ministry that is having a tremendous effect on the world for the cause of Christ, I find the person backing that ministry is always someone who has gone through some tremendous test, trial, or situation in his or her life....

The cost for being tremendously used of God is extremely high and there are many people who simply do not want to pay the price. There is a price to pay, a season to go through, but God has designed our lives so that the joys far outweigh the tears. Therefore, we must endure a season of pain for a season of gain.

(Quote from *Don't Die in the Winter,* Pages 71-72)

# QUESTIONS

1. Why do you think God designed us to endure a cross in order to gain a crown? Did He see beyond the cross? Do you?

2. What fruits of the Spirit are produced by seasons of pain? What attributes of the character of God do we have the potential to gain through difficult times?

3. How does a season of pain help keep our focus on God? Why is this necessary for those who have greater grace on their ministries?

4. What costs have you paid to be where you are today? How hard was it for you to pay the price? Are you ready to pay more and gain more?

5. The author tells us that "the joys far outweigh the tears." Have you found this to be true in your life? How does this fact bring witness to the power and compassion of God?

## MEDITATION

*"In our spiritual life there is always a season
of pain for a season of gain. In order for us to gain
a greater anointing and a deeper commitment for what
God has called us to do, there must be a season of pain"*

(Don't Die in the Winter, Page 71).

*How does God help us prepare for a season of pain?
Search for Scriptures that tell us what kind of attitude
we are to take during trials, and meditate upon these.*

# *His Word and My Prayers*

AND MAKETH MANIFEST THE SAVOUR OF HIS KNOWLEDGE BY US IN EVERY PLACE. FOR WE ARE UNTO GOD A SWEET SAVOUR OF CHRIST, IN THEM THAT ARE SAVED, AND IN THEM THAT PERISH: TO THE ONE WE ARE THE SAVOUR OF DEATH UNTO DEATH; AND TO THE OTHER THE SAVOUR OF LIFE UNTO LIFE (2 CORINTHIANS 2:14B-16A).

*M*y prayer life has been, and still is, like a cellular phone. With it I am able to maintain an open line of communication with God as I travel on my way. My map for life is the Word of God and prayer is my direct line of communication to God....

The threat of spiritual depression touches every believer's life....

A believer must "hold steady" and go on, or risk being consumed by the enemy....

When you find yourself in a state of spiritual depression, you are not yourself. Avoid the temptation to make rash decisions. Resist the urge to run. Instead, remember you have a mission in life. You have a divine assignment. You can bring about your own deliverance from a state of depression.

1. Practice smiling every day. A pleasant countenance frightens off the devil.

2. Understand that God sees you and knows everything you are going through.

3. Look to each day with renewed courage and strength.

4. Do something kind for someone else.

5. Sing yourself happy. The Lord's songs give the devil an earache.

6. Remind yourself that you belong to the Controller of the universe.

7. Look good! When you look good on the outside, you feel better on the inside.

(Quote from *Don't Die in the Winter,* Pages 75-77)

# QUESTIONS

1. Do you use the availability of prayer like a cellular phone? Are you in constant communication with the One who can help direct and spare you detours on your route? What do you need to do to increase your line of communication?

2. What is spiritual depression? How does this link with physical or emotional diseases? Have you ever been depressed spiritually? What were your symptoms? What helped you pull out of it?

3. How can prayer help during times of depression? Look up two or three psalms of David that express his depressed state or negative attitude. How did he talk to God? Were there words of praise in the psalm that helped him focus?

4. How can you bring about your own deliverance when you are depressed? What is involved in self-deliverance? Have you ever done this?

5. Look at the list of seven ways to bring about deliverance from depression. Which are easiest for you? Which are the most difficult? How can you use this list the next time you fight depression?

## ☜ MEDITATION ☞

*"Although we may be unaware of it, we
choose to be happy or sad. We either
live above the trials of this world, or we allow
those hardships to dictate and direct our attitudes"*

(*Don't Die in the Winter*, Pages 78-79).

*What dictates and directs your attitudes most often?
How can you create an environment around your head
and heart that will help you live above the trials you face?*

# *Persecution Is Preparation for a Miracle*

AND WE KNOW THAT ALL THINGS WORK TOGETHER FOR GOOD TO THEM THAT LOVE GOD, TO THEM WHO ARE THE CALLED ACCORDING TO HIS PURPOSE. FOR WHOM HE DID FOREKNOW, HE ALSO DID PRE-DESTINATE TO BE CONFORMED TO THE IMAGE OF HIS SON… (ROMANS 8:28-29).

*G*od has plans for you. He has a measure of the anointing He wants manifested in your life. God knows your spiritual potential and He knows your limit. He will not allow you to experience adversity any longer than necessary to fulfill His purpose for you.

What a comfort it is to know that God never allows us to be overloaded with tests and trials! When I go to have my car refueled, I have learned not to overload my gas tank. I used to pump gas until the meter indicated a full tank. Then I would force a few more gallons into the tank to make sure it was filled to capacity. I learned that this is both unwise and dangerous. Even so is our growth in God.

God knows your limit. He will allow only the struggles you need to bring out your full potential as a believer. God will allow just enough of a test to bring out His best in you. The words of an old gospel hymn by Roberta Martin gives encouragement:

"…you have the joy of this assurance. The heavenly Father will always answer prayer and He knows, I am so glad He knows, He knows just how much we can bear."

(Quote from *Don't Die in the Winter*, Pages 83-84)

# QUESTIONS

1. Do you know what measure of anointing God wants to manifest in your life? What do you think is your spiritual potential? What are the limits to your adversity? Is it comforting to know that God knows these things clearly, even if we are sketchy in our perceptions?

2. Have you ever told someone you were on overload? Why can't this be true according to what God promises about tests and trials?

3. How do you think God chooses what struggles we need to bring out our full potential as believers? If you had to select the types of trials that would be best for you, what would you choose? Would you be "safe" and easy on yourself or would you "overdose" and be too hard on yourself?

4. What is "just enough" of a test? How does God limit what you experience? How does He pull us out before we are on overload?

5. How do you know that your heavenly Father always answers your prayers? Is it easy for you to trust in His answer when it is "no"? When it is "wait"? How can we learn to rejoice in these answers the same way we rejoice when the answer is "yes"?

## ☙ MEDITATION ❧

*"Whenever God is about to perform a miracle
in your life, there will always be opposition and
persecution. Satan's goal is to abort God's will in your
life and he uses other people to accomplish his purpose"*

(*Don't Die in the Winter*, Page 83).

*Why does opposition and persecution prelude miracles?
How has satan used other people to accomplish his
purpose to oppose a miracle pending in your life?*

# Satan Had a Plan, but God Had a Bigger Plan

HE THAT DWELLETH IN THE SECRET PLACE OF THE MOST HIGH SHALL ABIDE UNDER THE SHADOW OF THE ALMIGHTY. I WILL SAY OF THE LORD, HE IS MY REFUGE AND MY FORTRESS: MY GOD; IN HIM WILL I TRUST (PSALM 91:1-2).

Satan hates people who are full of God and who are living in intimate fellowship with Him....

We can find comfort in the safety of God's protection if we learn several things about how satan operates.

1. The more you do for God and the greater the anointing you carry, the greater will be the effort of the enemy to discourage you.

2. Satan will buffet you in any way that he can.

3. The devil does not bother those individuals who are not a threat to his kingdom of darkness.

Nothing takes God by surprise. God always has somebody who will pray and seek Him....When God's people pray today, God moves. God cannot walk past a praying church. He will quiet the praises in Heaven to hear the prayers of one saint.

God's mercy is drawn to our difficult situations.... He is in our situation waiting for us to pray, to call on His name, and to seek Him. God is waiting for us to invite Him in. God will not impose Himself on our situation....

Persecution and hard times bring about the miraculous. Persecution gives us something to preach about. It gives us something to pray about.

(Quote from *Don't Die in the Winter,* Pages 85-86, 89-90)

## QUESTIONS

1. Why does satan hate people who are full of God and living in intimate fellowship with Him? Why doesn't satan target only those who have not yet reached the kingdom? How much does satan hate you?

2. How great is satan's effort to discourage you? Why does this strategy target those with the anointing of God?

3. How has satan buffeted you? Are there any patterns in his methods? What can help you block these attacks?

4. If satan is bothering with you, he deems you a threat. In what way do you threaten him?

5. Do you believe that when you pray, God moves on your behalf? Why does He wait for us to call on His name and invite Him into our situation?

## MEDITATION

*"The Word of God [is] a refuge in times of adversity
and persecution. God's promises [are] always a sure
word of encouragement in...valleys of pain and hurt"*

(Don't Die in the Winter, Page 91).


*What does a "refuge" mean to you? How does
the Word of God become a refuge? Do you readily seek
God's Word when you are in a valley of hurt and pain?*

# God's Word Continues to Confirm Our Persecution

LESSED ARE YE, WHEN MEN SHALL REVILE YOU, AND PERSECUTE YOU, AND SHALL SAY ALL MANNER OF EVIL AGAINST YOU FALSELY, FOR MY SAKE. REJOICE, AND BE EXCEEDING GLAD: FOR GREAT IS YOUR REWARD IN HEAVEN: FOR SO PERSECUTED THEY THE PROPHETS WHICH WERE BEFORE YOU (MATTHEW 5:11–12).

*S*truggles, strife, storms, and hard times give God an opportunity to show us who He really is. When storms rise, contrary winds begin to blow, and suffering comes, we must say with assurance that nothing will be able to "...separate us from the love of God, which is in Christ Jesus our Lord" (Rom. 8:39).

*Many are my persecutors and mine enemies; yet do I not decline from Thy testimonies* (Psalm 119:157).

*...bless them that curse you, do good to them that hate you, and pray for them which despitefully use you, and persecute you* (Matthew 5:44).

We need to encourage ourselves knowing that persecution is preparation for a miracle. "In all things we are more than conquerors through Him that loved us" (Rom. 8:37). Yes, "we are persecuted, but we are not forsaken; we are cast down, but we are not destroyed" (see 2 Cor. 4:9).

This is not the time to surrender or give up. God is about to birth you forth in your season. This is not the time to become depressed or to sing the blues.

The power of God gives us strength.
The Spirit of God gives us boldness.
The Son of God gives us health.
The saints of God give us hope.

(Quote from *Don't Die in the Winter,* Pages 92-93)

# QUESTIONS

1. How do struggles, strife, storms, and hard times give God an opportunity to show us who He really is? How do they show how much we trust God? What assurances do we receive from the Lord?

2. Take the following Scriptures and put your name in each one wherever appropriate. (Matthew 5:11-12; Romans 8:39; Psalm 119:157; Matthew 5:44; Romans 8:37; 2 Corinthians 4:9). Pray over these Scriptures and ask God to hide them in your heart.

3. Do you feel much like a conqueror? What does "more than a conqueror" mean? Does this describe you?

4. Where is the line drawn between "persecution" and "forsaken"? Where is it drawn between "cast down" and "destroyed"? Why are the differences between these conditions important?

5. Memorize the four statements at the end of this journal entry. Look at the equations they make: Power = strength; Spirit = boldness; Son = health; saints = hope. How can you realize these in your life in a greater measure?

## MEDITATION

*"The Church is indestructible, regardless
of what the enemy does. Jesus said that the gates
of hell would not prevail against it (see Mt. 16:18).
So we should not think it strange when
persecution and hard times come upon us.
If we endure, God promises a great reward"*

(Don't Die in the Winter, Page 91).

*Have you thought it strange when persecution
and hard times come your way? What rewards
does God promise you for your endurance?*

# Know Who You Are in God

**B**UT YE ARE A CHOSEN GENERATION, A ROYAL PRIESTHOOD, AN HOLY NATION, A PECULIAR PEOPLE; THAT YE SHOULD SHOW FORTH THE PRAISES OF HIM WHO HATH CALLED YOU OUT OF DARKNESS INTO HIS MARVELLOUS LIGHT (1 PETER 2:9).

## ☞ TODAY'S DEVOTION ☜

*K*nowing who we are in God is essential to preparation. Without this knowledge we react like spiritual orphans who do not have a home, provision, or privileges. There are three ways to learn about who you are in God:

1. Look at your reflection in God's divine mirror.

2. Learn what it means to be in the royal priesthood.

3. Allow the Lord to plant you in a Bible-believing church.

People see Jesus in our lives when we overcome adversity with the power of God. We become parables of Jesus Christ to the people we meet....

As you come to understand the reason for your adversity, your journey will have greater meaning. You will learn to appreciate your sojourn there....

Hurting people do not want to hear Scripture recited to them or have Bible tracts shoved in their hand. They want to know, "Have you been where I am? Have you felt what I'm feeling? If so, *how did you survive?*"

Our testimony strengthens others. But first, difficult times build strength in us. Strength produces endurance and endurance gives us a better testimony. Persecution is no longer an enemy. It is seen for what it is—preparation for a miracle.

(Quote from *Don't Die in the Winter*, Pages 94, 96-97)

# QUESTIONS

1. Why do we need to know who we are in God if we are to prepare successfully for seasons of adversity? How do we do this? How do we know if our preparation is successful or not?

2. What is the impact to others when the power of God is demonstrated through our adversity? How can we release the power of God so that it is the greatest thing others see?

3. How does our journey have greater meaning when we understand the reasons for adversity? Why does this impact our appreciation of the adversity?

4. Why do testimonies have greater impact than Scriptures, tracts, or sermons to many people? What do our testimonies do for others? For ourselves? For God?

5. Write out the last paragraph of this journal entry as mathematical equations. For example, "Our testimony = strength to others." What do you see in these equations? What encouragement do you receive?

## Meditation

*"If you want to be used of God, you must be prepared. If you miss God in your season, you will miss God's best"*

(*Don't Die in the Winter*, Page 93).

*What does this mean to you? Have you ever missed God in your season? Have you ever been prepared and were then able to receive God's best?*

# Opposition Is God's Opportunity

BE NOT AFRAID NOR DISMAYED BY REA-
SON OF THIS GREAT MULTITUDE; FOR THE
BATTLE IS NOT YOURS, BUT GOD'S. … YE
SHALL NOT NEED TO FIGHT IN THIS BATTLE: SET
YOURSELVES, STAND YE STILL, AND SEE THE SALVA-
TION OF THE LORD WITH YOU, O JUDAH AND
JERUSALEM… (2 CHRONICLES 20:15,17).

Opposition is not a time for us to back up, allow fear to overtake us, question God, or go back on our knees after we have heard from God. The devil always has a counterfeit for every authentic word that God speaks to our heart.

Opposition and opportunity go hand in hand, but even the opposition of the enemy can work positively in your life. Opposition will make you stand stronger and firmer in the things of God. You can allow opposition to strengthen your prayer life and cause you to search deeply and more consistently in the Word of God. What the enemy meant for evil, God can turn around and mean for good....

Many times God will allow a person to come into your life to oppose you. That person can turn out to be the greatest blessing in your life because the adversity will drive you to God. First Samuel 1 describes the opposition that Hannah received from Peninnah because she was barren. It drove her to agonize in prayer....

Joseph received opposition from his brothers as well. He knew part of God's plan and he made the mistake of sharing it with his brothers. We must be careful with whom we share God's revelation for our life. Sometimes people will oppose you just because God desires to bless you.

(Quote from *Don't Die in the Winter,* Pages 102-103)

1. Why do we often want to back up when opposition faces us? Why does fear play a major role in opposition? How have you overcome fears in your past? What does "standing still" mean?

2. Have you encountered opposition from the enemy that made you stand stronger and firmer in the things of God? How can opposition bring such results?

3. Have you had someone oppose you when you have been moving toward opportunity? Have you had other Christians oppose you? Family or friends? How can we avoid taking this opposition personally and seeing beyond it into the spiritual realm?

4. Have you let opposition become a tool to strengthen your prayer life? Have you used it to become familiar with Scriptures and let God's Word penetrate your heart? What good can evil bring to you?

5. Do you identify with either Hannah or Joseph in the examples given? Have you had people bring opposition to you in either of these ways? What was the outcome?

# MEDITATION

*"Opposition and opportunity work hand in hand. They are married to one another. You will not find one without the other. Wherever God opens a tremendous door of opportunity and blessing, there will always be opposition from the enemy to keep you from going through it"*

(*Don't Die in the Winter*, Page 101).

*Have you personally experienced opposition and opportunity working hand in hand? What situations have you faced when God brought opportunity to your door? Were you able to press through the opposition?*

# Learn How to Encounter Opposition

NO WEAPON THAT IS FORMED AGAINST THEE SHALL PROSPER; AND EVERY TONGUE THAT SHALL RISE AGAINST THEE IN JUDGMENT THOU SHALT CONDEMN. THIS IS THE HERITAGE OF THE SERVANTS OF THE LORD, AND THEIR RIGHTEOUSNESS IS OF ME, SAITH THE LORD (ISAIAH 54:17).

*T*here are six things that are essential when we encounter opposition:

1. We must understand what opposition is.

2. We must ask the Lord to help us remain positive.

3. We must take a stand against the enemy.

4. We must do what God tells us to do.

5. We must pray for our enemies.

6. We must seek God in faith.

God is not the author of bad things. He is the giver of all good and perfect gifts (see Jas. 1:17). It is the goodness of God that leads us to repentance. God's will for us is always good. When you see opposition in your life, you must understand that God will use it to bless you....

Do not hold on to bitterness against the people who oppose you. Look beyond individuals. Know that it is the enemy using people to oppose you. Pray for them because they may be unaware that they are instruments of satan (see Mt. 5:44)....

If you have made a total commitment to the Lord in your life, God will give you a glimpse of the magnitude of satan's plan to keep you from being effective as His instrument. The good news is that "whatever the devil means for evil, God means for good."

(Quote from *Don't Die in the Winter*, Pages 103-104, 106)

# QUESTIONS

1. Examine the six actions essential when encountering opposition. Evaluate yourself according to these six areas. Which are easiest for you to do? The most difficult? Where do you need to grow before the next opposition comes?

2. So many people wonder where God is when tragedies occur. If He is not the author of bad things, why do these things happen? How does James 1:17 answer this question for us?

3. It is often difficult to forget the hurtful things that people say and do who oppose you. How can you look beyond their words and actions? Who is the author of the opposition? How can prayer change them and also you?

4. Ask the Lord to give you a glimpse of satan's plan to keep you ineffective. Ask Him to reveal the weakest parts of your character that need to be strengthened in order to withstand the wiles of the enemy. What are these weak areas? Look up Scriptures that speak to each one.

5. Do we have to wait for the end of opposition to see God's hand at work? Why or why not? What will help us gain perspective while we are going through opposition and not just after the fact?

# ☙ MEDITATION ☙

*"As a result [of opposition], I have a deeper appreciation of the sunshine of God's blessings—and you will too. Remember, life is 10 percent how you make it and 90 percent how you take it"*

(*Don't Die in the Winter*, Page 106).

# *Seasonal Transitions*

B ELOVED, THINK IT NOT STRANGE CON-
CERNING THE FIERY TRIAL WHICH IS TO
TRY YOU, AS THOUGH SOME STRANGE
THING HAPPENED UNTO YOU: BUT REJOICE,
INASMUCH AS YE ARE PARTAKERS OF CHRIST'S
SUFFERINGS; THAT, WHEN HIS GLORY SHALL BE
REVEALED, YE MAY BE GLAD ALSO WITH EXCEED-
ING JOY (1 PETER 4:12-13).

# ❧ TODAY'S DEVOTION ❧

*I*n order to move from one life season to another, change must occur. Every transition encourages our spiritual wholeness and growth. This growth brings glory to God....

At every grade level in school, we usually have to submit to a test or some kind of assessment that reveals, "This is what I know. This is what I've learned. This is my preparation for the next level." We need to be able to say, "I can handle what is coming next."

Before we are promoted in God, we have to be tested. The test itself does more for us as individuals than one who administers the test. The test indicates to us how well we are prepared to go on, to move up in God, and to take on greater responsibility....

When you want to be blessed by God and used of God, you must go through something to prove your durability....Yet when the struggles come and our heart is breaking, God wants to know if we can still sing, teach, preach, and serve through the tears. Can we do what God has called us to do when there is trouble all around us? Then, and only then, our true level of commitment and faith is revealed.

(Quote from *Don't Die in the Winter*, Pages 109-110)

## QUESTIONS

1. What life seasonal changes have you experienced? How have transitions encouraged your spiritual wholeness and growth? How has your growth brought glory to God?

2. How well do you handle tests? Do you clam up and sweat? Do you find yourself prepared? Do you find your endurance fading? Just as we prepare for tests in school, how should we prepare for spiritual tests?

3. Think through your times of testing. Have you embraced them as a necessary part of your growth? Have you seen them as the step toward promotion?

4. How is durability tested on manufactured products? How does God test your durability? Why is durability such an important factor in a quality Christian?

5. When testing comes, why do many of us want to run and hide and regroup instead of continuing in our service despite the tests? Why is continuing in our call and ministry during trials so important to our witness?

## MEDITATION

*"In order to be promoted in the things of God or to come into our best season, we must go through times of tempting and testing"*

(Don't Die in the Winter, Page 109).

*What does this mean to your life? What promotions have come to you as you have gone through times of tempting and testing?*

# *Accept and Encourage Change*

AND NOT ONLY SO, BUT **WE GLORY IN TRIBULATIONS** ALSO: KNOWING THAT TRIBULATION WORKETH PATIENCE; AND PATIENCE, EXPERIENCE; AND EXPERIENCE, HOPE: AND HOPE MAKETH NOT ASHAMED; BECAUSE THE LOVE OF GOD IS SHED ABROAD IN OUR HEARTS BY THE HOLY GHOST WHICH IS GIVEN UNTO US (ROMANS 5:3–5, EMPHASIS ADDED).

Change is the very essence of life. To resist change is to work against life; it's like trying to swim against the current. When we accept change, however, and encourage it, we are in the flow of life....

Then, instead of working against those changes, we work with them and cry out to God, *"What is it that You want me to learn from this experience? What do You want to show me about myself through this circumstance or situation?"* This attitude puts us in the flow of our season, and makes the best of that particular time....

Paul tells us that in the future we will *"become,"* but until then we must *"overcome."* This means we will experience difficulties that help us grow. To boast in our sufferings means to rejoice in suffering. We rejoice in suffering, not because we like pain or deny its tragedy, but because we know God is using life's difficulties and satan's attacks to build character. The problems we encounter will develop our patience, which in turn will strengthen our character, deepen our trust in God, and give us greater confidence about the future. You probably find your patience tested in some way every day. Thank God for these opportunities to grow.

(Quote from *Don't Die in the Winter,* Pages 111-112, 115)

# QUESTIONS

1. What does it mean to "glory in tribulations" in Romans 5? Are we to enjoy suffering? Are we to put on a happy face when inside we are gloom and doom? What are we to do?

2. How has accepting change helped you to move in the current of God's flow of life? Have you ever worked against the current? What was the outcome? Have you used the current to your advantage? How does this help us?

3. Our attitude during change is critical to making the best of our struggles. Why is this true? What questions should you ask the Lord at the onset of change? What questions should you ask after the change has been made?

4. How have you overcome your struggles and challenges? What have these made you become? What parts of your character have been developed through change?

5. Look up two or three Scriptures about patience. How is patience an integral ingredient of getting the best out of our tribulations?

# MEDITATION

*"God allows us to go through changes so
we can grow up. Every hardship, burden, problem,
pain, sickness, fear, and disappointment that comes
into your life is an opportunity for you to grow"*

(Don't Die in the Winter, Page 114).

*Are you grown up? Do you act like
a spiritual grown-up? Do your challenges help
you grow, or do you push them away like a child?*

# Accept Your Destiny

I F ANY OF YOU LACK WISDOM, LET HIM ASK OF GOD, THAT GIVETH TO ALL MEN LIBER-ALLY...AND IT SHALL BE GIVEN HIM (JAMES 1:5).

*I*f you are frightened…
  If you are losing heart…
  If you will not go where God tells you to go…
If you will not do what God tells you to do…
If you will not say what God wants you to say, then God
will find Himself a people *who are willing to obey Him.*

There is no excuse because the same God who waved the
waters of the earth, that cut out the ocean, who hung the sun,
moon, and stars, who says, "I am that I am…"—this same God
says to you, "*You are the sons and daughters of Zion.*" (See Exodus
3:14.)

I am disturbed whenever I hear believers say, "Never question God." Surely God, in His infinite wisdom, can endure questions from man…. Believers do not have to grope in the dark,
hoping to stumble upon answers. We can ask God for wisdom to
guide our choices….

It begins with respect for God, leads to right living, and
results in increased ability to hear His voice. To learn God's will
in any difficult situation, we must:

1. Read His Word.

2. Ask Him to show us how to obey His Word.

3. Do what He tells us to do.

(Quote from *Don't Die in the Winter,* Pages 116-118)

1. Have you ever been frightened or lost heart? Have you ever determined not to go the direction God is telling you to go? Has God ever passed over you to another because of your inability to obey?

2. Many Bible characters questioned God. Some did well and others did not. Compare Mary's questions to the angel who visited her with Zechariah's questions. What made them different? What attitude must we have when we question God?

3. David questioned God frequently in the Psalms. Skim through the Psalms and write down some of these questions. Are there ones you frequently ask? What were the answers to David's questions? Are they the same answers God gives to you?

4. When we feel like we are groping in the dark, stumbling for answers, what should we do? What light is at the end of our tunnel? How can we find the direction toward that light?

5. How does our respect for God bring us an increased ability to hear Him? Do you find the three directives above to be easy or difficult to do in a time of testing? When your devotions feel "dry," should you still have them?

## MEDITATION

*"When difficulties arise, we all are tempted to ask God, 'Why?' This is especially true when we are living lives of faith"*

(*Don't Die in the Winter*, Page 117).

*The question "why" may show we have an "entitlement mentality." What are you entitled to as a Christian?*

# God's Perspective

A ND LET US NOT BE WEARY IN WELL DOING: FOR IN DUE SEASON WE SHALL REAP, IF WE FAINT NOT (GALATIANS 6:9).

*W*hen God allows you to go through the valley of the shadow of death, and it is so dark that you cannot see your hand in front of your face, God will teach you how to praise Him. You can praise Him in spite of whatever situation comes in your life. Every valley experience offers you a lesson in praise....

Problems help us, they do not hinder us.
They bless us, not burden us.
They develop us, not destroy us.
They cleanse us, not corrupt us.
They refine us, not ruin us.
They mold us, not break us.
They train us, not torture us.

Seasonal transitions will come and go in our lives. Change is inevitable. Remember, it is how well we are prepared for that change that will make the difference. "Examine yourselves, whether ye be in the faith; prove your own selves..." (2 Cor. 13:5). Are you prepared:

1. To accept change in your life?

2. For radical commitment?

3. To manifest God's strength as you struggle?

4. To accept your destiny?

5. To confess, "He's still God"?

6. To keep praising God?

7. To hang in there?

8. To view difficulty from God's perspective?

9. To pray, "Thy kingdom come"?

We say it often: "Thy kingdom come, Thy will be done." Now we must have the faith to believe it for our own lives. It is time to totally surrender to God's love and let the Holy Spirit have His way with us.

Quote from *Don't Die in the Winter*, Pages 121-123

# QUESTIONS

1. Has God taught you how to praise Him in the midst of a dark situation? Have you learned to praise Him in spite of whatever situation comes into your life? What lessons in praise have you learned through your valleys?

2. Look at the list of what problems accomplish versus what they do not do. Rewrite the list of things that they do not do (i.e. hinder, burden, etc.) and then rewrite a corresponding list of what they do accomplish (i.e., help, bless, etc.). How can the problems we face move from the negative side to the positive? Use this list whenever a problem comes your way to encourage your heart into God's perspective.

3. Athletes test their skills, strength, and endurance by putting themselves to the test. Is this what Second Corinthians 13:5 is speaking of? How can we prove ourselves?

4. Look at the nine questions to determine if you are prepared for your next test. Which ones seem easy to you? Which are more difficult? What preparation must you make to increase your perspective from God's point of view?

5. What does "Thy kingdom come, Thy will be done" mean to you? Rate your faith on believing this prayer. Why does this take surrender on your part? What does this surrender look like?

## MEDITATION

*"Diamonds do not sparkle unless they
are cut. Roses do not release their fragrance
unless they are crushed. A seed does not
take root unless it falls to the ground, and stars
do not shine until the darkest hour. We need
to view difficulty from God's perspective"*

(*Don't Die in the Winter*, Page 122).


*Does the analogy of a diamond, a rose, or
a seed best describe your latest difficulty? What
do you believe is God's perspective on that difficulty?*

# God's Holding Pattern

FOR TO BE CARNALLY MINDED IS DEATH; BUT TO BE SPIRITUALLY MINDED IS LIFE AND PEACE. BECAUSE THE CARNAL MIND IS ENMITY AGAINST GOD: FOR IT IS NOT SUBJECT TO THE LAW OF GOD... (ROMANS 8:6-7).

## TODAY'S DEVOTION

*T*here is a season in our spiritual growth when God places us in a holding pattern....

We can't move to the left or the right....When we're deep down in the midst of a difficult situation, God can talk to us. When He has our undivided attention, He can show us things about ourselves that we might not otherwise have seen.

Here are a few of God's holding patterns

1. When you are sick in your physical body and you have prayed, but God has not healed you yet, you are in a holding pattern.

2. When you are having problems with your children and you have put them on the altar, but God has not delivered them yet, you are in a holding pattern.

3. When you have been praying for the salvation of a loved one and they have not been saved yet, you are in a holding pattern.

4. When you are in a broken relationship and you have given it over to God, but it has not been restored yet, you are in a holding pattern.

5. When the doors slam shut before you can knock on them, you are in a holding pattern.

(Quote from *Don't Die in the Winter,* Pages 127, 130)

1. Why does God place us in holding patterns? Have you ever been in one? Describe your feelings and situation. What kind of vulnerability did you feel at this time?

2. Why can God speak to us when we are in holding patterns? How does this bring us to the point where He receives our undivided attention? What has He shown you in such times about your character?

3. Look at the five descriptions of holding patterns. Think of an example for each one (if possible), remembering the situation you were in and what brought you to that point.

4. From the examples you gave above, which seemed the most difficult for you? Why? What part of your character did God address through this holding pattern? Do you feel you have grown because of it?

5. What do you think you might do to prepare for a future holding pattern so that you will recognize what it is and be able to focus on God more quickly than in the past?

# MEDITATION

*"God calls every one in the Body of Christ
to do a work for Him. Each believer has an
assignment in the Kingdom of God. Sometimes
our work for the Lord is simple, easy, and
comfortable. Or it may be difficult, distasteful,
time-consuming, and confining. The
choice belongs to God, not us"*

(*Don't Die in the Winter,* Page 128).

*If you were to tell someone your primary
assignment in the Kingdom of God, what
would it be? Has your assignment been
simple and easy at times? Has it been difficult at
other times? What description would you give it today?*

# Obedience Brings Blessings

AND BE NOT CONFORMED TO THIS WORLD: BUT BE YE TRANSFORMED BY THE RENEWING OF YOUR MIND, THAT YE MAY PROVE WHAT IS THAT GOOD, AND ACCEPTABLE, AND PERFECT, WILL OF GOD (ROMANS 12:2).

We cannot run from God and also expect Him to bless us.

We cannot defy God and expect Him to bless us.

We cannot disobey God and expect Him to bless us.

We cannot ignore God and expect Him to bless us.

We cannot sin against God and expect Him to bless us.

We cannot run from God, because there are no mountains that are high enough, valleys that are low enough, rivers that are wide enough, rooms that are dark enough, or places that are hidden enough from Him.

There are three things to remember when we find ourselves in a holding pattern:

1. The pattern has a purpose.

2. The pattern has a plan.

3. The pattern has a process.

When you belong to God, your life has a purpose. That purpose is to glorify God and to obey Him in all that you say and do....

The pattern not only has a purpose, but the pattern has a plan....

God has a blueprint for the life of every believer. Every decision we make, everything we do, and everything we say is interwoven into that design. When we go our own way, do our own thing, and do not follow His plan, God's design for our life is interrupted.

(Quote from *Don't Die in the Winter,* Pages 131-132)

## QUESTIONS

1. Have you ever tried to run from God? Why do many of us still seek His blessing even as we are trying to run away?

2. Do you tend to defy God, disobey God, or ignore God when you disagree with His will? What results can you expect from any of these reactions? Then why do we still pursue our own way?

3. When we go our own way, we act as if God is limited in vision, perspective, and time. We reduce Him to our own limitations. What does this do to our potential blessings? Why do we need to break free from the "limits" we put on God?

4. Look at the three things to remember about holding patterns. Remembering these could keep you from what kinds of negative attitudes and thought patterns?

5. Think through your life since you became a Christian. Does it reveal God's purpose for you? Does it show a pattern of His involvement with you?

# MEDITATION

*"The pattern for the life of every child of God
has a purpose. Because it has a purpose, every
divine detail plays a part in God's design for your life"*

(*Don't Die in the Winter*, Page 132).

*Explain these statements in terms of your own life.
Think on how God's purposes have been revealed in you.*

# Is God Trying to Tell You Something?

CREATE IN ME A CLEAN HEART, O GOD; AND RENEW A RIGHT SPIRIT WITHIN ME (PSALM 51:10).

*E*very pattern not only has a plan and a purpose, but it has a process as well. That process must run its full course. When we disobey God and stand in direct opposition to God's plan for our life, we are subject to His judgment.

But the purpose of God's judgment is not revenge; it is for correction. Disobedience sets a process of correction and discipline in motion....

The purpose of God's judgment is always correction.

Every pattern has a process, but thanks be to God, the process is not permanent. When we effectively learn what God wants us to learn, God brings His judgment to an end.

We are waiting on God and God is waiting on us. We can cut God's judgment short when we effectively learn what God wants us to learn....

Ask Him for these five things:

1. To help you.

2. To hold you.

3. To mold you.

4. To help you to hear only His voice.

5. To prepare you for what He has called you to do.

Many people experience bouts of depression in the middle or toward the end of winter....They feel as if spring will never come, even though they know that winter never lasts forever....

Winter does not last forever. Spring is always just around the corner.

(Quote from *Don't Die in the Winter,* Pages 133-135)

# QUESTIONS

1. Why is the process of a pattern just as important as the plan and purpose of that pattern? What do processes inherently have that provide us opportunities to grow?

2. If we reject the process God wants us to go through, why is this rejection considered disobedience that can lead to rebellion? How does God view these types of actions? Have you ever rejected God's process for a pattern in your life and received a sharp rebuke from Him?

3. Why does God judge us? Do you think He withholds mercy and grace when He brings His justice to bear? Why or why not? What purpose does judgment have?

4. How can we effectively cut God's judgment short? Look at the five things we should ask from God. Explain why each is important.

5. Have you ever been depressed during a long spiritual winter? What made you forget that spring would be coming? What are some ways out of depression?

## MEDITATION

*"We need to understand that God is trying
to tell us something—that the best is yet to come and
that whatever we are going through will not last forever"*

(*Don't Die in the Winter*, Page 134).

*What comfort does this bring to you
or future difficulties? Do you think you are
prepared to look beyond the circumstances
and gain a perspective from God's vantage?*

# *How Strong Are We?*

B LESSED IS THE MAN THAT ENDURETH TEMPTATION: FOR WHEN HE IS TRIED, HE SHALL RECEIVE THE CROWN OF LIFE (JAMES 1:12A).

*W*hen we have to endure a tremendous amount of opposition and persecution, we need to hold steady until the season changes....

We need to:

1.  Encourage one another until we win.

2.  Never jump ship before we get to harbor.

3.  Never get off the horse before the race is over.

4.  Never throw in the towel before the game ends.

You cannot lose if you do not quit....

We all like to think of ourselves as being as strong as the tree planted by the rivers of the water in Psalm 1. Now a tree trunk can look healthy on the outside....

But if a bolt of lightning comes along and strikes that tree, you will see the true nature of the inner parts of the tree.... If lightning strikes your life...will you be able to hold steady under the pressure?

If we break, spiritual instability is exposed. This reflects an inconsistent prayer life, a lack of true interest in the Word of God, and a weak relationship with God....

If you are being tested right now, it means that God has something in store for you.... If you can take it, you can make it. But if you are not willing to go through the test, then there is no promotion in God.

(Quote from *Don't Die in the Winter*, Pages 135-137)

# QUESTIONS

1. How well have you been able to hold steady during times of opposition and persecution? Have you found it to be easy or difficult? How do we develop the endurance that is needed for such challenging times?

2. Look at the five things we need to do to hold steady. Which are the easiest for you to do, generally speaking? Which is the most difficult? Why? What kind of strengthening do you need to be able to hold steady during your next problem?

3. How strong is your tree? Are your roots deep? Is your trunk sturdy and receiving regular nourishment? Are you protected by other trees around you? Are your branches healthy and full of life? Are you ready for a lightning bolt to reveal what is hidden inside of you?

4. What characterizes spiritual instability? Have you ever found yourself to be spiritually unstable? Why do we desire to do the opposite of what God wants when we are spiritually unstable?

5. Are you being tested right now, or do you know someone who is? What do you think God has in store? Why is willingness to go through times of testing a prerequisite for promotion in God?

# ☙ MEDITATION ☙

*"God says that these trials are not
for our destruction, but these trials are
for our development. He desires to bless us and use us,
but He has to know that we can handle the blessings"*

(*Don't Die in the Winter*, Page 137).

*Do these statements counter the world's logic? Have
you found this to be true in your own life? How?*

# God's Word Is a Two-Edged Sword and a Mirror

THOU THROUGH THY COMMANDMENTS THAST MADE ME WISER THAN MINE ENEMIES... (PSALM 119:98).

*G*od's Word is a ready weapon, like a two-edged sword. This sword will jump up in your hand when you need it to fight against temptation. We need to put the Word on every situation....

The best way to defeat an enemy is to know his strategy and to plan a counterattack. Knowing God's Word makes one wise to satan's tactics....

Knowing what God says about the subtlety of the enemy makes you privy to satan's devices. Study the Word of God to destroy your enemy and bring his surrender....

The Word is also like a mirror. When we get up in the morning and look in the mirror, we might not like what we see, but the mirror does not lie. So we groom ourselves and do what we can to face the world.

We look untidy, so we wash and moisturize and rub and pat dry. We shave off and rub on and pluck out. We do whatever has to be done in order to face the world.

God's Word will always show us what we look like. It can prepare us to meet the challenges of everyday life if we read it early in the morning. The Word enables us to spiritually groom ourselves.

(Quote from *Don't Die in the Winter,* Pages 139-141)

# QUESTIONS

1. Have you ever seen or handled a heavy broadsword? Without training, it can be a hinderance rather than a powerful weapon. How do we need to be trained in using God's sword, the Word of God, so that it will be a powerful weapon for us?

2. How does the Word of God reveal satan's tactics? Have you understood what the enemy was trying to do because God revealed something in His Word to you? What do we do with this type of revelation once we have received it?

3. Have you ever thought of satan surrendering to you? Does this happen each time we defeat his purposes and maintain our walk with God?

4. How has God's Word been a mirror to you? What are some of the things it has revealed? Have you seen positive aspects of who God has made you to be, as well as those aspects that need changing? What are some of these aspects?

5. How does God's Word help us to meet the challenges of everyday life? Why is there no separation between our sacred and secular lives? How are we to "groom ourselves" for the day?

## MEDITATION

*"As you go through your winter season of adversity, allow God's Word to 'warn you.' The best defense is a good offense"*

(Don't Die in the Winter, Page 140).

*Have you ever experienced a warning from God's Word? How does this happen? How can you be on the offensive instead of the defensive when trials come your way?*

# Out of Sync—Out of Season

THE LORD GOD hath given me the tongue of the learned, that I should know how to speak a word in season to him that is weary... (Isaiah 50:4).

## ⌐ TODAY'S DEVOTION ⌐

It is vital to know which particular season we are in. If we are "out of season," then almost everything that we put our hand to will fail. The Lord gives us a measure of anointing, and we are equipped to carry out only what God wants us to do during a particular season....

God, in His infinite wisdom, has a *best time* to bring you out of your winter season. When your time is fully come, there will be no doubt that a miracle is being performed in your life. If your deliverance from pain and adversity is premature, someone else or something else might get the glory. God wants all the glory to go to Him....

If you are "out of season," you are not "in season." When you find yourself "out of season," you must:

1. Get on your knees.

2. Stay before the Lord.

3. Ask Him for divine direction.

4. Search the Scriptures and allow the Word of God to speak to you.

5. Ask God to show you His timing for your life.

6. Ask Him to give you a spirit of patience. We tend to want to follow our own time schedule, but we need to wait for His.

(Quote from *Don't Die in the Winter*, Pages 145-148)

# QUESTIONS

1. Do you know what particular season you are in right now? Have you ever been "out of season" and seen that everything you did seemed to fail? How is God's anointing connected to your seasons?

2. How is God's "best time" to bring you out of a winter important? What is available if you wait for this best time? What might happen if you do not? How have you seen these principles worked out in your own life?

3. Look at the six things you should do when you are out of season. Which of these are easy for you to do during adversity? Which are more difficult? Why?

4. How do you find Scriptures that can speak to your situation? Do you use a concordance, a promise-type book, or your regular devotional readings? Do you memorize the Scriptures that can bring your deliverance? What other resources are available?

## ☙ MEDITATION ❧

*"God also has a specific time set to bring*
*us to full fruition in our work for Him.*
*It is incumbent upon us, therefore, to discover*
*God's divine schedule for our lives"*

(Don't Die in the Winter, Page 146).

*What have you learned about the timing*
*of God in your life thus far? Have*
*you discovered God's divine schedule?*

# He Prepares Us for Every Good Work

AND WHEN HE PUTTETH FORTH HIS OWN SHEEP, HE GOETH BEFORE THEM, AND THE SHEEP FOLLOW HIM: FOR THEY KNOW HIS VOICE. AND A STRANGER WILL THEY NOT FOLLOW, BUT WILL FLEE FROM HIM: FOR THEY KNOW NOT THE VOICE OF STRANGERS (JOHN 10:4-5).

*T*hings do not *just happen* in the life of a believer. Your life is not an experiment.... After you accept Jesus Christ and are saved, God does not scramble to figure out what He is going to do with you, now that you belong to Him.

Every movement of your life is prepared and established by God Almighty....This does not mean that we live in a robotic existence or that our life is predestined without regard to our personal choices or our own will....

It is not enough to accept Jesus Christ as Savior. We must also make Him Lord. Making Christ Lord involves making Him the ruler and controller of our life....

For those who dislike any kind of control in their life, this is not an easy thing to do. But the moment you ask Jesus to come into your life, God puts a plan into action. He has a design, a blueprint, and an agenda for your life. The Holy Ghost gets right on the job and sets the plan in motion. Yes, you might veer off the path or lose direction. You might go off on a tangent, or find yourself temporarily diverted, sidetracked, or detained. But, by and by, God will intervene in every situation and set your feet on the right course.

(Quote from *Don't Die in the Winter*, Pages 150-151)

# QUESTIONS

1. How does hearing God's voice affect the way Christians see the world around them? How do believers become clear as to what the Shepherd's voice sounds like?

2. If "things do not *just happen* in the life of a believer," why do Christians still believe in chance circumstances or luck? Why do we often take on a victim mentality concerning the events around us? What should our mind-set really be?

3. How does the preparation and establishment of your life by Almighty God allow room for your free will? When you stray from the way God has ordained, what happens?

4. Think back to when you made Christ Lord of your life. How easy was it for you to give up control? Why? How does trust come in to play in terms of making Jesus Lord over your life?

5. How does God correct our course when we get off track? How has He done this in your life? Have you found it easy or hard to get back on course? Why?

## MEDITATION

*"We have to know the voice of God*
*for ourselves. Then when the voices of 'experts'*
*come at us, we can discern the difference between*
*the good intentions of other people and God's voice"*

(*Don't Die in the Winter,* Page 149).

*How do you recognize the voice of God?*
*How should we use counsel from others?*
*Who are your wise counselors?*

# *Where Are You, Lord?*

F OR HE HATH SAID, I WILL NEVER LEAVE THEE, NOR FORSAKE THEE (HEBREWS 13:5B).

*G*od examines our situation and says, "I'm going to make it part of My plan." This does not mean that God's plan is canceled out or that His plan changes. It simply means that anything and everything that happens to you, from the moment you accept Christ until the moment you die, God will work it out for your good....

God allows us to go through situations in our own lives because we need substance to our testimony....Then we can go to someone else who needs a word of encouragement....

Everything, good and bad, is part of the intricate design that results in the beautiful mosaic of a life totally committed to Him....

We may "feel" like evil has the upper hand, but remember, God is in control of everything! God is sovereign!...

Never lose hope—God will overcome evil. Yes, we live in a sinful and fallen world, and as long as this world exists there will be evil to contend with. But this is not the time to give into the temptations and pressures around us. It is just for a season....

When we are faithful to the Lord, God is faithful to us. He gives us power and strength to endure our tests and our trials. His peace helps us to go through the opposition and the persecution that the enemy brings upon us.

(Quote from *Don't Die in the Winter,* Pages 151-154)

## QUESTIONS

1. God masterfully weaves even our negative situations into His master plan. How does He do this? In light of this fact, what should we understand about those actions we've committed that we are ashamed of?

2. What is your testimony like? What situations have you faced that can speak to others in similar circumstances? Have you built the glory of God's sovereignty into your testimony?

3. Why is the issue of God's sovereignty so critical when we go through challenges or when the world around us seems to be falling apart? How does His sovereignty bring us a sure victory?

4. How do you find comfort when trials come your way? Do you do special things that bring you comfort? Do you eat particular foods? Where are we supposed to go to be comforted? Is this easy for you to do?

5. Think of a time when God gave you power and strength to endure a test or trial. What made the difference for you? Think of a time when God gave you peace during opposition or persecution. How did His peace bring you through to a new season?

## MEDITATION

*"Although God will never leave us
or forsake us (see Heb. 13:5), sometimes
we 'feel' like He does. Have you ever been so
discouraged that you wanted to quit? We are
tempted to give up, compelled to surrender, driven
to our wits' end, and almost persuaded to forsake it all"*

(Don't Die in the Winter, Page 152).

*Think through times of discouragement
in your life when you wanted to quit.
How has God brought you to Him at these times?*

# Persistence in Prayer

ASK, AND IT SHALL BE GIVEN YOU; SEEK, AND YE SHALL FIND; KNOCK, AND IT SHALL BE OPENED UNTO YOU: FOR EVERY ONE THAT ASKETH RECEIVETH; AND HE THAT SEEKETH FINDETH; AND TO HIM THAT KNOCKETH IT SHALL BE OPENED. ...HOW MUCH MORE SHALL YOUR FATHER WHICH IS IN HEAVEN GIVE GOOD THINGS TO THEM THAT ASK HIM? (MATTHEW 7:7-8,11)

## Today's Devotion

*G*od has promised us [that] He hears us and answers us. However, He does so in His own time. There is a season for answered prayer, just as there are seasons for rain and snow....

When it looks like all hope is gone, set yourself in a season of praying and staying like Joseph did. When you cannot find your way, when you feel like giving up, when everybody tells you what you're doing cannot be done—pray and stay. When they laugh at you, talk about you, and walk out on you, pray and stay!

Delays are not denials. Rather, they indicate that you are not in your "due season of blessing." But your season is coming.... If you hold on to what God has called you to do in this life, the Word promises that there will be a great and tremendous reaping (see Gal. 6:9).

This "reaping" is a full manifestation of the Holy Spirit in your life. God will cause people to bless your life. He will cause your gift to make room for you. God will open doors of opportunity for you. People will be blessed as you exercise your ministry. You will reap tremendous blessings if you do not grow weary during divine delays. Remember, a sturdy oak is an acorn that held its ground!

(Quote from *Don't Die in the Winter,* Pages 156, 158)

# QUESTIONS

1. Matthew 7:7-8,11 is not a quick-release remedy for those things that we do not like. What do these verses mean to you? Are there conditions to achieve these results? If so, what are they?

2. What does a "season for answered prayer" look like? How does this work for us as believers? Do we pray and then stop praying, or do we constantly badger God with our requests until He answers, or is there something else?

3. List the negative circumstances Joseph experienced from the time he dreamed the dream of rulership until he became ruler under Pharaoh. What characterized his walk with God? What type of prayers did he pray? What does this say to you in your times of challenge?

4. Read Galatians 6:9. What are we to hold on to in order to receive God's promise? What kind of rewards do we receive? What do you think stops us from receiving our reward?

5. Describe a time of "reaping" in your life. What challenges brought you the substance to be a strong laborer in God's field? What rewards were in it for God's Kingdom? Were there any rewards for you?

## MEDITATION

*"It is His time. We need to hold on. It
will not be much longer. The battle will soon be over;
the course will soon be finished; and the race will soon be
won. Joseph learned this lesson. He held on to God's Word"*

(*Don't Die in the Winter*, Page 157).

*Has your life struggled against the race you run?
Do you see delays as costly to your resources and
time rather than character-building advantage points?*

# Be Not Weary in Well Doing

FOR MY THOUGHTS ARE NOT YOUR THOUGHTS, NEITHER ARE YOUR WAYS MY WAYS, SAITH THE LORD. FOR AS THE HEAVENS ARE HIGHER THAN THE EARTH, SO ARE MY WAYS HIGHER THAN YOUR WAYS, AND MY THOUGHTS THAN YOUR THOUGHTS (ISAIAH 55:8-9).

*A*ny kind of development requires a process....

There is a systematic process that every student must go through as he advances in life. This is true in our spiritual lives as well. Have you passed the test?

1. We must be discipled under consistent, firm, stable, and godly teaching. God's Word tells us to study to show ourselves approved unto God. We must be workmen who need not be ashamed (see 2 Tim. 2:15). The Word of God needs to be sown deep in our spirit.

2. There is a time when we are before the Lord to discover our particular area of ministry and specific calling in the Body of Christ.

3. We need a time of sitting under capable mentorship in our calling. This is where we watch an anointed role model function in a ministry.

4. Then there is a time when we birth forth fully in our own ministry to carry out what God has called us to do. I call this our "due season."

A season does not care about human opinion. A season has no respect for what a person thinks or does not think. When it is your time and your season to come forth, people can talk about you, deny your calling, refuse to license you, vote you out, call you crazy, sit you down, shut you up, and shut you out. But when it is your time and your season to come forth, nothing can stop you.

(Quote from *Don't Die in the Winter*, Page 165)

# QUESTIONS

1. If you could highlight some of the systematic spiritual education you have experienced over the years, what would you see? What tests did you pass? What ones did you fail?

2. Read Second Timothy 2:15. In what "subjects" are you being discipled? Would there be any areas that, if examined, would cause you shame?

3. Do you know your specific ministry of calling to the Body of Christ? If so, how did you learn this? If not, what do you need to do to discover this?

4. Who are your role models? Who are your mentors? What do you want to receive from these people? How can you be sure you will get what you want?

5. Why can't man stand in the way of your "due season"? Why do we think that those in authority have more power than God does to promote us or hold us back? How is this incorrect perception broken?

## MEDITATION

*"It is important to know when you are
in your season. The 'signs of the times' are
understood through a consistent study of God's Word"*

(Don't Die in the Winter, Pages 162-163).

*Has this been true in your experience?
How do you know when you are in season?*

DAY 36

# Discover Your Life Purpose

ND I WILL BRING THE THIRD PART THROUGH THE FIRE, AND WILL REFINE THEM AS SILVER IS REFINED, AND WILL TRY THEM AS GOLD IS TRIED: THEY SHALL CALL ON MY NAME, AND I WILL HEAR THEM: I WILL SAY, IT IS MY PEOPLE: AND THEY SHALL SAY, THE LORD IS MY GOD (ZECHARIAH 13:9).

## ◈ TODAY'S DEVOTION ◈

*W*e have been gifted by God for a certain purpose, and it should be our life pursuit to discover our purpose and fulfill it.

We are tremendously blessed of God and we do not recognize it. We look for material things and God sends spiritual blessings. There are five ways to know that you are in your due season:

1. Your prayer seed comes to fruition.

2. You stand back and watch the power of God manifest.

3. Doors will open in your life.

4. You will be laughing at the devil.

5. Spiritual warfare becomes very subtle.

Things that need to happen will happen without your having to push, pull, and politick. You will simply stand back and watch God perform. God will bring everything and everybody that you need into your life. You will meet people, by God's design, who have just the talents that you need to carry out the work He has assigned to you....

It is good to write your prayer seed down. Put it in a visible place and keep this request as a focus. Keep praying. No one reaches their season without prayer. When you see this seed coming to fruition, you know that you are in your due season.

(Quote from *Don't Die in the Winter,* Pages 166-167)

# QUESTIONS

1. What is your life pursuit? Have you been gifted for your call? Can others see your gifts and your call easily?

2. Why do we often not recognize God's spiritual blessings? How can we be in a position where recognition will come easily?

3. Look at the five ways to know you are in your due season. Have you experienced each of these? At what time in your life did you experience any of these? Did any come together at the same time?

4. Have you ever stood back and watched God perform, bringing your gifts forward and fruit bursting forth from your hands? When people have such experiences, what is at work?

5. Do you have a prayer seed today? Write it down and keep it in a visible place so that you can continue to focus on it in prayer.

# MEDITATION

*"We are gifts to the earth. Our task in this life is to discover our God-given gifts so we can be a blessing to others. Our due season is that particular time when our gifts come to full fruition"*

(*Don't Die in the Winter*, Page 166).

# In Due Season

A MAN'S GIFT MAKETH ROOM FOR HIM, AND BRINGETH HIM BEFORE GREAT MEN (PROVERBS 18:16).

# ☙ TODAY'S DEVOTION ☙

*I* [once] stood in my pulpit, exhausted, overworked, and stressed out. But I remember that day with sweetness now because my winter season has passed. Winter will come again, as all seasons do, but I know how to prepare myself now. I can recognize winter's approach.

Now I can nurture and shepherd those 14 new converts who gave their heart to the Lord [that day]. When their winter season arrives, I am ready to go with them and minister hope in the midst of adversity.

The words of my testimony have life. Flesh and bone cling to every sermon I preach. Dead people need a Living Word. The blood of Christ gives every word life, and so the message lives.

I have entered a season of continuous praise for what God has done in my life. Others have died in winter. They lie frozen, cold, and stiff in the chilly winds of adversity. They gave up. But I endured and I survived. Today I thrive in the midst of God's blessings. The smile on my face is genuine. The love in my heart is sincere. The excitement with which I serve God is real.

I have endured my winter.
I have survived the wilderness.
I have come out of the valley.
I am in due season.

(Quote from *Don't Die in the Winter,* Pages 173-174)

# QUESTIONS

1. How does a "man's gift maketh room" in due season? Have you experienced the truth of this Scripture? Is there a formula for this, or how do we trust it will happen?

2. The author believes that she will be able to recognize winter's approach as it comes again. How will she do this? How will you? Recognition is key to preparation. How will you prepare?

3. How will you be able to help others through their winters? What transferable concepts have you learned that you can share with others who are in need of a hope?

4. Do the words of your testimony have life? How do you share the Living Word? What message do you preach?

5. What is a season of "continuous praise"? How does someone come into such a season? What kind of excitement does this season bring to you?

## ⌇ MEDITATION ⌇

*"Suffering in and of itself is not a privilege. However, when we suffer as a result of faithfully representing Christ, we know that our message and example have an effect and that God considers us worthy to represent Him"*

(*Don't Die in the Winter*, Page 174).

## DAY 38

# *Stir Up Your Spirit*

WHEREFORE I PUT THEE IN REMEM-
BRANCE THAT THOU STIR UP THE
GIFT OF GOD, WHICH IS IN THEE BY
THE PUTTING ON OF MY HANDS (2 TIMOTHY 1:6).

*S*uffering for our faith does not mean we have done something wrong. In fact, the opposite is often true—it verifies that we have been faithful....

The terms of *winter, wilderness,* and *valley experiences* are used interchangeably to describe difficult places in our Christian experience. They are one and the same, and we all have to pass through them.

As you come to understand the reason for your winter season, your journey will have greater meaning. Not only will you learn to appreciate your sojourn there, but God also will strengthen your testimony with words that will glorify Him.... Just as I looked carefully at my own adversity to understand my winter season, you too must look carefully at your own life and hardship to understand your spiritual seasons....

*You will marvel at the faithfulness of God. Begin to prepare for winter. Fortify yourself!* You will laugh, you will cry, you will question, and you will think. And if you "hold on" and "endure," when the season passes, you will "grow."

"Stir up" your spirit and hear what the Lord is saying in your life. Provoke your prayers and focus your heart in the right direction.

(Quote from *Don't Die in the Winter,* Pages 11-12, 174-175)

## QUESTIONS

1. When you are in seasons of suffering, have you felt that you did something wrong to earn your challenges? When might this be true? When might it not be true?

2. Why is understanding the reason for your winter important? When is the most beneficial time to know the reason for winter? Why?

3. How can we appreciate our sojourns in winter? What process is needed for us to understand our spiritual seasons?

4. How do we "fortify" ourselves for winter? What are some of the emotions you have experienced in winter? What are the fruits of the Spirit you have gained because of your winters?

5. How do we "stir up" our spirit? Why is this necessary in order to wake out of the slumber of self-pity and a victim mind-set? How can stirring your spirit elicit prayer and a correct focus?

## MEDITATION

*"God has helped me in my wilderness walk.*
*I marvel at the faithfulness of God.*
*I greet each day with anticipation"*

(*Don't Die in the Winter*, Page 174).

# God's Weather Channel: Spring and Summer

TEACH ME, O LORD, THE WAY OF THY STATUTES; AND I SHALL KEEP IT UNTO THE END. GIVE ME UNDERSTANDING, AND I SHALL KEEP THY LAW; YEA, I SHALL OBSERVE IT WITH MY WHOLE HEART (PSALM 119:33-34).

# ☙ TODAY'S DEVOTION ☙

*G*od's Word provides food for thought and sustenance for living. Knowing the Word gives us guidance through the seasons of life. Every verse offers spiritual insight to the one who prayerfully searches and uncovers truths, truths that bring comfort and understanding during a season of adversity.

## Spring Season

### Visibility

*Neither give place to the devil* (Ephesians 4:27).

### The Forecast

*This is the day which the Lord hath made; we will rejoice and be glad in it* (Psalm 118:24).

### Showers of Blessings

*...if I will not open you the windows of heaven, and pour you out a blessing, that there shall not be room enough to receive it. And I will rebuke the devourer for your sakes...* (Malachi 3:10-11).

## Summer Season

### Sunrise/Sunset

*For from the rising of the sun even unto the going down of the same My name shall be great...* (Malachi 1:11).

### Weather Wisdom

*The steps of a good man are ordered by the Lord: and He delighteth in his way. Though he fall, he shall not be utterly cast down: for the Lord upholdeth him with His hand* (Psalm 37:23-24).

### Heat Wave

*We are troubled on every side, yet not distressed; we are perplexed, but not in despair; persecuted, but not forsaken; cast down, but not destroyed* (2 Corinthians 4:8-9).

(Quote from *Don't Die in the Winter*, Pages 185-186)

1. How have you used God's Word to help you during seasons of your life? How does His Word help you in a season of spring? A season of summer?

2. Look through the "Spring Season." Why is "Visibility" important at this time? We can get caught up in "The Forecast," expecting better weather than in our winter, but what should our thanksgiving be during this time?

3. "Showers of Blessing" sounds very refreshing! Why do we need to focus on the Source and substance of our blessings and not just the outward blessings themselves?

4. Look through the "Summer Season." The beginnings and endings of each day should be focused where? We can marvel at the sunrises and sunsets we see, but we need to marvel more at each spiritual sunrise and sunset in our lives. What are these?

5. The weather in summer can be refreshing but can also be oppressive. How can you be wise in your preparation for each type of spiritual weather that comes? How can you prepare for a heat wave?

## MEDITATION

*"Just as we prepare ourselves for seasonal changes
in the natural, we must also clothe ourselves in the
righteousness of God's Word during seasonal changes"*

(*Don't Die in the Winter,* Page 185).

*How do we clothe ourselves in the righteousness
of God's Word? Memorize the spring and summer
Scriptures provided as part of your devotional regimen.*

# God's Weather Channel: Fall and Winter

For in the time of trouble He shall hide me in His pavilion: in the secret of His tabernacle shall He hide me; He shall set me up upon a rock. And now shall mine head be lifted up above mine enemies round about me: therefore will I offer in His tabernacle sacrifices of joy; I will sing, yea, I will sing praises unto the Lord (Psalm 27:5-6).

# ❧ TODAY'S DEVOTION ❧

*I*n winter, everything is cold, drab, bleak, and still. But winter is the necessary hardship that we must pass through to get from fall to spring.

In the realm of spiritual things, a similar season lies between the fall of past expectations and the birth of new hopes and blessings....

Because I have been in the depths of pain, darkness, and satanic attack, I have a deeper appreciation of the sunshine of God's blessings—and you will too.

## Fall Season

### Today's Outlook

*For the eyes of the Lord run to and fro thoughout the whole earth, to show Himself strong in the behalf of them whose heart is perfect toward Him...* (2 Chronicles 16:9).

### Highs and Lows

*Therefore, my beloved brethren, be ye stedfast, unmoveable, always abounding in the work of the Lord, forasmuch as ye know that your labour is not in vain in the Lord* (1 Corinthians 15:58).

### Atmospheric Pressure

*...When the enemy shall come in like a flood, the Spirit of the Lord shall lift up a standard against him* (Isaiah 59:19b).

## Winter Season

### Storm Warning

*Be sober, be vigilant; because your adversary the devil, as a roaring lion, walketh about, seeking whom he may devour* (1 Peter 5:8).

### Wintry Skies

*I will lift up mine eyes unto the hills, from whence cometh my help. My help cometh from the Lord, which made heaven and earth* (Psalm 121:1-2).

### Windchill Factor

*...weeping may endure for a night, but joy cometh in the morning* (Psalm 30:5).

(Quote from *Don't Die in the Winter*, Pages 11-12)

# QUESTIONS

1. How have you used God's Word to help you during seasons of your life? How does His Word help you in a season of fall? A season of winter?

2. Look at the "Fall Season." How does our spiritual "Outlook" affect how we proceed in our growth? How do we learn to weather the spiritual "Highs and Lows" we face?

3. What kinds of "Atmospheric Pressure" affect you spiritually? Where are your weakest points? What might you do to prepare for the winter ahead by recognizing and strengthening yourself in your weakest points?

4. Look at the "Winter Season." How can we recognize that a "Storm Warning" is being broadcast to us? When things seem gray in our spiritual "Wintry Skies," how can we remain focused?

5. What "Windchill Factors" have tripped you up so that you could not see beyond the day and its problems? How can we press through to see spring ahead?

## MEDITATION

*"Commit such passages to memory. These truths
will bless you in your season....Be encouraged
as you tune in to God's divine weather channel"*

(*Don't Die in the Winter*, Page 185).

*Use the Scriptures in the Fall and Winter Seasons
as memory verses during your devotions. Get prepared
for winter by "stocking up" on the Word of God now.*

# Don't Stop Here!

As a follow-up to this 40-day journal, we suggest you continue with Dr. Hunter's 30-day devotional (see *Don't Die in the Winter*, pages 175-181). This exercise will cement the principles from the Word and bring you to a new level of preparation for future seasons ahead.

## Day 1

I live in God's time, not my own. God lives in eternity. He has no beginning and no end (see Rev. 22:13). He always was, is, and shall be. Time is only a piece of eternity, just as a slice of an apple pie is a piece of the whole pie.

Time is limited by its boundaries. My life is limited by time. I have a beginning and an end. I live in the slice and God lives in the pie.

I can see only my space of time. God sees my eternal existence and He operates according to the limitless expanse of eternity. Therefore, God's will for my life will bless me and benefit me for eternity. God has looked ahead. He has an eternal plan. His plan may not seem to be in my best interest for the moment, but God is least concerned about the moment. God lives in eternity.

## Day 2

Israel suffered many hardships and persecution. God's people often felt alone and deserted by God, but He knew that His people had to be prepared to live in total dependence upon Him. He took Israel through seasons of change and growth.

Hardships and problems teach me to depend upon God. Strife causes me to focus my attention on God. God has arranged the seasons in my spiritual life in order to produce Christlike character in me (see Jas. 1:2-4).

## Day 3

Some seasons are longer than others according to the level of strength and commitment that God wants to build in me. Am I willing to endure the long winter? (See Jas. 1:12.)

## Day 4

God made provision for Israel in the wilderness. When my season of hardship and persecution is long and difficult, God always makes provision for me. One of His covenant names is "Jehovah Jireh." It means "the God who supplies our needs." I am thankful for His provision (see Phil. 4:19).

## Day 5

God orders and directs my steps because I have asked Him to. Psalm 37:23 says, "The steps of a good man are ordered by the Lord: and He delighteth in his way." Although I do not always know where I am going, I know who is leading me there.

## Day 6

Sometimes I want to skip certain steps of my growth. I want to do as much as I can for God, as quickly as I can. However, I cannot grow faster than God permits. I cannot rush God (see 2 Pet. 3:8).

## Day 7

I remember when I was a small child. I know what it is like to grow physically, to learn, and to develop into a mature adult. I do not want to remain a spiritual child. I am willing to grow, to learn, and to develop in the things of God. I know this will take time. God has time; therefore, I have time (see 1 Cor. 13:11).

## Day 8

Sometimes I still act like a child. I want my own way. I want to say "no." I manipulate others with my emotions. I know that there are areas in my life that need further growth. I have to decide. Do I want to grow up? (See Heb. 5:12-13.)

## Day 9

God wants me to grow to spiritual maturity; therefore, He is taking me through seasons to bring me to the place of maturity in Him (see Eph. 4:13-15).

## Day 10

When I reach the time that I am ready to "blossom forth" in my work for Him, I must move out or I will miss my best season. (See John 9:4.)

## Day 11

An apple tree can blossom forth at any season of the calendar year if it is kept in a hothouse (protected from storms, insects, and cold temperatures), but that is not the way God intended for apple trees to grow. God does not want to keep me in a Christian "hothouse." He plants me where I am able to experience the natural conditions of life (see 2 Pet. 3:18).

## Day 12

God has arranged the physical world so that flowers show forth their best in the spring and summer. Corn and wheat show forth their best in the fall. Evergreens are beautiful in the winter. Every area of nature has a season in which it can show forth its best. So do I. (See Eph. 2:10.)

**Day 13**

God has planned a special season for me. It will be a time when He can use me for His glory. His love will shine through me in a special way. I am anxious for this season, but I am willing to wait. I want to be like the rose that is ready to burst into bloom. I do not want to be a rosebud that dries up because it is not ready for the sunshine. (See Eccles. 3:11a.)

**Day 14**

I need to know the "signs of the seasons" so I can have the mind of God and use each season for maximum growth. Therefore, I must begin to pay attention to the circumstances and changes in my life from a bibilical perspective. (See Eph. 4:23.)

**Day 15**

God directs the timing of all nature. The flowers bloom in His time. The trees drop their leaves in His time. The planets readjust themselves in His time. God directs the timing of all things in my life as well. (See Eccles. 3:1.)

**Day 16**

A hothouse tomato is not as red, juicy, and palatable as a tomato grown in the warm July sunshine. A hothouse rose cannot compare with the regal beauty of a garden rose. I can create artificial conditions in my life if I want to. Do I really want to? (See Titus 3:8.)

**Day 17**

If I am not aware of the seasons of growth and the qualities that God wants to produce in me, I will begin to create artificial qualities that do not have substance or depth. I will end up with surface strength, superficial wisdom, and a shallow character. (See John 15:4.)

**Day 18**

If my life lacks depth and wisdom, my ministry will be ineffective. It will not change lives because my own life has not yet been fully changed. (See John 14:15.)

**Day 19**

God is not finished with me yet. I must allow Him to continue to work on me according to His own schedule. If I do not, I will find myself walking and operating in areas for which I am totally unprepared. (See John 15:5.)

**Day 20**

There is great value in abiding in Jesus (see Jn. 15). If I abide in Him, then I will act like Him, look like Him, and love like Him. He is the Vine. I am a branch that looks like it belongs to the Vine.

**Day 21**

I know that I will prosper, regardless of the season. God has prosperity reserved for me. He gives me all that I need, regardless of the circumstances in my life (see Phil. 4:19).

**Day 22**

I will not allow the enemy to have a foothold in my life. He has no power over me. God has not given me a spirit of fear. I have a sound mind. I have power. I have love. I have self-control. (See 2 Tim. 1:7.)

**Day 23**

I will praise God at all times and give Him thanks, for this is His will concerning me (see 1 Thess. 5:18). I will not allow the enemy to buffet my life with self-pity. He is an empty mist that has no power over me.

**Day 24**

God's Word is profitable for me. It equips me for every good work and trains me in righteousness (see 2 Tim. 3:16). My growth is dependent upon the Word of God in me. I rely on His Word in every season.

**Day 25**

I am dressed in garments of salvation and praise. The full armor of God covers me and protects me from the evil one. I am prepared to stand in the evil day (see Eph. 6:10-17).

**Day 26**

Seasons of pain are for my gain. Those who want God to use them must pay a high price. God has designed situations in my life so the joys far outweigh the tears, the pain, the tests, and the trials. I can endure this season because I know that spring is coming. (See Ps. 34:19.)

**Day 27**

Instead of allowing fear to overtake me, I will use this opportunity to let God demonstrate His power over anything the enemy tries to do to me. Opposition is God's opportunity in my life. (See 2 Tim. 1:2.)

**Day 28**

Changes have taken place in my life that are difficult to embrace and accept. Yet I know that I must move on. I must keep growing. Every experience in my life is helping me to discover my divine potential and life purpose. (See 2 Tim. 1:9.)

**Day 29**

I want to be like a tree planted by the waters. I will not walk in the counsel of the ungodly or stand in the way of sinners. I refuse to sit with the scornful.

My delight is in God's Word. I will meditate on it day and night. I will bring forth fruit in my season. My leaf will not wither and whatever I do will prosper. (See Ps. 1.)

**Day 30**

I am not afraid of the winter.

I refuse to die.

I know that spring is coming.

I hear the birds chirping.

I hear the bees buzzing.

The sun is beginning to beam down on my head.

I refuse to die because I know my season is coming.

# Bishop Millicent Hunter

*The Cathedral* Baptist Worship Center
4790 James Street
Philadelphia, PA 19137
Phone (215) 289-7879
Fax (215) 289-1704
www.thebaptistworshipcenter.org

TWO SERVICES
EVERY SUNDAY MORNING

WORSHIP SERVICE 9:00 AM

CHILDREN'S CHURCH 9:00 AM
WORSHIP SERVICE 11:00 AM

*Bishop Millicent Hunter*
*Founder & Pastor*

## DON'T DIE IN THE WINTER

Why do we go through hard times? Why must we suffer pain? *In Don't Die in the Winter* Dr. Hunter explains the spiritual seasons and cycles that people experience. A spiritual winter is simply a season that tests our growth. We need to endure our winters, for in the plan of God, spring always follows!

**ISBN 0-7684-2294-9**

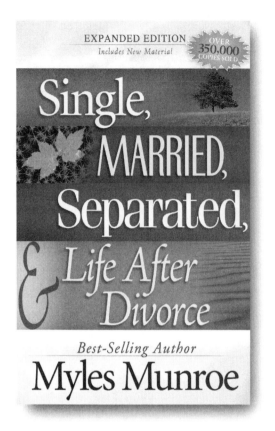

**EXPANDED EDITION**
*Includes New Material*

OVER **350,000** COPIES SOLD

# Single, MARRIED, Separated, & Life After Divorce

*Best-Selling Author*
# Myles Munroe

## SINGLE, MARRIED, SEPARATED, & LIFE AFTER DIVORCE

Myles Munroe, deals with the complicated and emotion-laden issues of relationships, lack of loving relationships and the severance of relationships in this powerful little book. Looking at the volatile issue of divorce and its aftermath, Dr. Munroe shares the counsel he has given to thousands of people.

**ISBN 0-7684-2202-7**

**Available at your local Christian bookstore.**

**For more information and sample chapters, visit www.destinyimage.com**

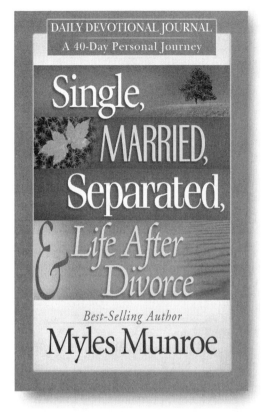

## SINGLE, MARRIED, SEPARATED, & LIFE AFTER DIVORCE DAILY DEVOTIONAL JOURNAL

A 40-day personal journey providing a daily study devotional, and journal based on Dr. Munroe's best-seller. Stepping out of the single life into the married life is a big step and Myles Munroe offers tried and tested truths enabling men and women to survive the change from singlehood to marriage. Unfortunately, as more and more marriages are ending in divorce there is a desperate need for answers to the haunting questions that trouble the divorced person.

**ISBN 0-7684-2239-6**